Still Speaking of Nature

excelsior editions

AN IMPRINT OF STATE UNIVERSITY OF NEW YORK PRESS

Still Speaking of Nature

further explorations in

the natural world

Bill Danielson

Photographs by Bill Danielson.

Published by
STATE UNIVERSITY OF NEW YORK PRESS
ALBANY

For information, contact
State University of New York Press, Albany
www.sunypress.edu

Production and book design, Laurie Searl
Marketing, Fran Keneston

LIBRARY OF CONGRESS CATALOGING-IN-PUBLICATION DATA

Still speaking of nature : further explorations in the natural world / Bill Danielson.
       p. cm.
   ISBN 978-1-4384-3599-2 (hardcover : alk. paper)
   1. Natural history—New England. 2. Seasons—New England. 3. Natural history—New York (State)—Adirondack Mountains. 4. Seasons—New York (State)—Adirondack Mountains. 5. Danielson, Bill, 1940– I. Title.
   QH104.5.N4D36 2011
   508.74—dc22

                                                      2010023367

    10   9   8   7   6   5   4   3   2   1

Contents

v

Introduction

When I was a boy, I was surrounded by nature. I grew up in the town of Amherst, Massachusetts, in a house that was beautifully situated in the landscape. The house lot itself was not particularly large, but the topography surrounding it gave the woods a certain endless quality that still resonates within me to this day. To the immediate east and north of the house ran a curving and ever-deepening ravine formed in the sandy soil by a small, ephemeral stream, and for many years the farm on the other side of the ravine was uninhabited. Even after the property of the farm was eventually purchased, the ravine acted as a barrier that prevented the new neighbors from feeling like they were too close.

This ravine served as a playground for my brother and sister and me. The stream was dammed innumerable times and tiny impoundments that seemed to get a little larger and more ambitious with every passing attempt were established by our own department of public works. We used shovels to move mud and sand around, and sticks found on the ground to add reinforcement to the structure. Beaver dams were our inspiration, and I can remember how, even as a child, I was so very impressed with what beavers could accomplish. I think the one element that the beavers added to their dams that we could not was patience. We could manage to invest an hour or two in each of our dam-building projects, but we never spent every waking moment fixated on the idea of stopping the water. We were children, after all.

The ravine was also a major thoroughfare for travel between our house and that of the Cushings. The road that ran in front of our home was well paved and had a rather high speed limit. My mother didn't like the idea of young kids walking near it if we didn't have to, but the ravine seemed like a perfectly reasonable alternative, so that was how we traveled. We were as at ease in those woods as Robin Hood would have been in Sherwood Forest, and with every passing year we got to know the lay of the land better and better. This was particularly useful to any of us who engaged in a rousing game of "ball tag." The rules of this game, invented by Tom Cushing, were simple. All you needed was a Nerf football and a yard. If you were "it," you had to nail someone with the football. If you weren't "it," you had to run like hell. At some point the game spilled out of the Cushings' yard and into the ravine, and to this day I have vivid memories of running for my life and closing in on unworthy opponents through those trees.

The stream running through the ravine eventually emptied into a pond not too far from my house. I say "not too far" now, but as a kid it seemed like a treacherous journey through Mirkwood Forest itself. We avoided following the stream and always circumvented the wetlands by way of the drier uplands. The pond was a feature of an old farm that had also been abandoned. Much more interesting was the abandoned sandpit that also resided on this property. It seemed huge, and the walls of the pit (about 20 feet in height) seemed like the walls of the Grand Canyon. The mining of sand must have been only recently halted because the walls were so vertical. This made for ideal nesting sites for a colony of bank swallows that called the sandpit home, and for many years their nest holes perforated the sandbanks. After a time, however, even the swallows abandoned the sandpit, but I have never really understood why. We never hurt or molested the birds in any way, but perhaps erosion took its toll, for one year the entire area was simply deemed unacceptable and the swallows were gone, never to return.

Across the street from my house there was an undeveloped lot that provided access to the Holyoke Range State Park. I lived right across the street from Mt. Norwottuck, and the trails and roads through the Park were heavily traveled by my friends and me. We would visit an old Boy Scout campsite on the side of the mountain, or climb to the top of the exotically named Rattle-snake Knob. We spent hours in and around the Horse Caves, and of course there was the summit of Norwottuck itself. The first bit of exposed rock offered an amazing view to the north. My house was plainly visible, as was the entire town of Amherst. You could see landscape features in the towns of Pelham, Montague, Leverett, Sunderland, and Hadley in the foreground, and the Green Mountains of Vermont on the northern horizon. A walk of an additional 100 yards to the actual geological summit of the mountain brought you to an old fire tower that was removed many years ago. When it was still in place, we could climb to the top and get a 360° view of the Pioneer Valley itself. The skyscrapers of Springfield and Hartford were visible to the south, and what appeared to be endless forests stretched off to the east and west.

As luck would have it, my family also made an annual trip into the forests of the Adirondacks. There was a Girl Scout camp called Camp Little Notch that was nestled into some 2,800 acres of rugged mountain forests, and for one magical week every year my family was able to occupy this camp with no one else around. We plied the waters of the camp's crystal clear lake for hours at a time in pursuit of largemouth bass, perch, and sunfish. At night, with flashlights in hand, we would walk to Flat Rock and search the shoreline for rock bass. The various campsites were referred to as units and were gifted with magical names like Sleepy Hollow, Timagimi, Pine Point, Sherwood Forest, and Tall Timbers. Each unit had its own feeling, and each left an indelible mark in my memories. The most vivid of those are from my teenage years when I was able to work at the camp for two entire summers. I learned the most about the property in that time and learned to cherish the solitude of our family week even more than I would have thought possible.

The woods and mountains surrounding my childhood home, and the forest, lake, and mountains of Camp Little Notch served as the cradle that nurtured my personal connection with Nature. As a kid I was aware of Nature's importance and variety, but what I lacked was a meaningful body of knowledge about how Nature worked. I can remember sitting in my grandmother's house and looking through her copy of *Peterson's Field Guide to the Birds*. As I flipped through the pages, I gazed (with awe) at the birds that surely existed out there somewhere, but that I had never seen. I was filled with a desire to learn as much as I could, so when I was ready to go to college, I enrolled in the wildlife biology program at U-Mass, Amherst. There I started the lifelong process of observation and study that have so wonderfully enriched my life. I will never forget the day I saw my first black-and-white warbler and realized that all of those mysterious birds from my grandmother's field guide were actually real. All I needed was some knowledge and understanding.

That's where this book comes in. My personal connection to Nature was started with exposure, but refined with knowledge. Personally, I am very interested in seeing wild places protected, and to my mind that requires knowledge. You cannot care for something that you don't know about. So every week for the past thirteen years I have tried my best to encourage a love of Nature in the readers of my various newspaper columns. I try to engage my readers with stories of events occurring right outside their windows, and I always encourage people to get out and see things for themselves. I even have a special column for children that is designed to encourage imagination and artistic expression in my younger readers. The essays contained herein represent a snapshot of the hundreds of columns that I have written over the years, and I hope that you can feel the love for Nature that I try to convey. If I can help you learn something you didn't know before, or care about something you never really considered before, then I have accomplished what I set out to do.

SPRING

Spring Rain

We humans are odd creatures. We fixate on the beginnings and endings of things so much that we even feel the need to impose our contrived schedules on Nature itself. We are driven by an unexplainable urge to categorize things, and we cannot rest until we have everything sorted out. The problem for us is the fact that Nature marches to its own beat. This keeps us unsettled, literally restless, and it may be a contributing factor to our amazing achievements as a species. Nature keeps us moving.

Take, for instance, the notion of spring. The very sound of the word evokes powerful images in our minds. We think of warmer temperatures that allow the perfume of damp earth to waft on the breeze. We think of every pigment on Nature's palette strewn across verdant fields in a riot of color. We think of the collective voice of the avian fugue rejoicing in the aftermath of winter. But the riot takes time to muster itself, and the fugue needs time to clear its collective throat. Spring is a work in progress, but we humans are driven to constrain it. We need to announce an opening date, whether it is accurate or not, and so we decided on the vernal equinox. Most years this is March 20, but leap years do cause their problems and they force the opening of spring to be delayed until March 21.

The problem with assigning an arbitrary date to such a fluid season is the fact that despite our planning, organizing, and scheduling, we don't know when spring will actually arrive. Spring is a diva, and she will not be rushed. She will appear in her own good time, but she will send many a tantalizing clue that she is on her way. Rather than just winking into view, she will ever so seductively materialize into existence. Long after we have seen her face and heard her voice for the first time, we will suddenly realize that she has been with us for quite a while.

I mentioned earlier that spring was a fluid season, and that was no accident. Spring is best identified with liquid water. After the biting cold of the long dark winter has solidified all but the swiftest-flowing waters, spring surrounds the landscape in the merciful warmth of her embrace and allows the waters to begin to soften. It starts out slowly, as it does every year, and then it grows. I'd like to say that my awareness of this phenomenon is due to my own personal intellect, but that would be boasting just a little too much. There are always signs that spring is on her way, but like the first few drops of spring meltwater, it is often difficult to identify these signs as part of the great spring flood that is to follow.

In January the owls start singing. There are three species of owls that call my neighborhood home, but in January I will hear

Ripples spread as a gentle rain falls on a rural pond.

only the great horned owl. Why is this? Well, there are actually two reasons. First, there is the simple interaction of the effects of weather on the observer (that would be me). Great horned owls are big birds with loud, deep voices—so deep and so loud that you can even hear them from inside your house. Since winter is cold enough to keep most people inside at night (including me), it stands to reason that I'd hear a great horned owl and not necessarily the others. This is the easiest explanation for the owl songs I hear in January.

Much more complicated is the fact that owls start their courtship in mid winter. This may seem amazingly early for such an event, but it must be remembered that owls tend to be rather large birds, and they require more time to mature than any of the small migratory birds that we are more familiar with. The largest of the owls—the great horned owls—have the most growing to do, so the parents start courting in January. Owls don't really build nests so much as they refurbish the preexisting nests of crows and hawks, so they only need about a week to get things in order. Eggs are laid at the beginning of February, and then the great gamble commences.

Owls understand that spring is a fickle flirt. They know that the prediction of her arrival is not something that can be done with any great precision, so they hedge their bets. Unlike robins or cardinals, warblers or catbirds, owls incubate their eggs in such a manner as to produce a staggered hatching event. This is achieved simply by incubating eggs as soon as they are laid. Robins and cardinals nest so much later in the season that they can afford to lay eggs and leave them unincubated until the last egg of the clutch is in place. Smaller birds produce eggs once a day, so the first egg may be left for several days, in stasis, before incubation finally begins. Once the final egg is laid, incubation commences and will not be interrupted until all of the babies hatch out at basically the same time. Owls do not have this luxury, however. Unattended eggs would surely freeze, so they must be kept warm at all times to protect the embryos within. Owls also don't necessarily lay an egg every day. So by the time the first egg hatches, there may be many days to go before the last baby emerges from its shell.

This is all because no one can truly predict the arrival of spring. The staggered hatching of owlets from their eggs is an insurance policy against bad timing. Little owls that hatch into a world that is still cold and snowy may not survive, whereas their younger siblings, still safe in the confines of their shells, will be spared. Sometimes a week can make a big difference and the babies that hatch out later will find the world a nicer place to be. The slightly smaller barred owls will compensate for their shorter growing times and wait until the beginning of March to start laying eggs. The little screech owls will wait until the end of March, after the human observance of the beginning of spring, to lay their eggs. All three species are attempting to time the greatest hunger of their new families to coincide with the greatest abundance of baby mammals that will fill the landscape. Even for owls, March seems too soon for spring.

Sooner or later, the cold will start to subside and the snows will start to disappear. The drip, drip, drip of meltwater is the herald of spring, but the first spring rain is her fanfare. Many of spring's actors start to take the stage long before her full glory is established, and each of them is like a drop of water melting off the landscape. The grackles appear . . . drip. The red-winged blackbirds appear . . . drip. The brown-headed cowbirds appear . . . drip. The flood is not fully formed, but you can sense it building. The turkey vultures appear . . . drip, drip. The mallards start pairing off and exploring every little puddle they can find . . . drip, drip. The skunk cabbage flowers poke their heads out above ground . . . drip, drip. The flood is beginning to take shape, but it is still little more than a trickle.

Then I hear the season's first killdeer calling from the lower field . . . gurgle. The crows start building nests in the shelter of spruces and pines . . . gurgle. And, as always, there will eventually come that special night when I hear the call of a woodcock from my lower field . . . gurgle, gurgle. But this is all preamble. This is the equivalent of listening to an orchestra warm up before a performance, and this cannot start without the establishment of rhythm—the rhythm of raindrops falling from the sky and hitting first ice, but later the softer surface of open water.

Without that first spring rain you cannot hope to start the arpeggio that is the arrival of spring.

As a naturalist I spend a great deal of my time making the sorts of observations that keep me well informed of this rhythm, and many years ago I started keeping a field journal of the events of every season in every year. Looking through them from time to time allows me to keep my expectations realistic; to allow myself patience in the face of a fashionably late spring, and to avoid outright panic in those years when spring is unquestionably tardy. I see words printed on the page and I feel that I can trust them because, after all, I wrote them. I don't always manage to make the same kinds of observations every year, because my life is just as fluid as Nature itself, but there was one year when I managed to capture the essence of the first spring rain in words. I shall now take those few phrases and expand upon them in an effort to convey to you the sights and sounds of that day—to create a sense of place, as it were.

For me, the epitome of spring rains fell in Altamont, New York, on April 17, 2007. I woke up that morning to a gray sky that made no false promises of sunshine. It was already raining, and I could see a thin layer of fog above the snow in my field. The rain was not particularly heavy; in fact it was so gentle as to be almost comforting. The world was quiet, but there were signs that it was starting to stir.

I ate a quick breakfast, grabbed my camera, and got into my car. This was not a morning for the radio, so I cracked my windows and headed slowly down the road with only the occasional cycle of the wipers to keep me company. It reminded me so much of similar car trips from my early childhood; happy, quiet, and contemplative. I traced the track of a raindrop down the window with my finger as I had so often done as a boy.

I was on the lookout for anything, but not anything in particular. Nature is everywhere around us, but we still have to be in the right place at the right time. As it happened that morning, the right place was a small, secluded pond that I had never noticed before. In this case, it was the last remnants of the winter ice that caught my eye.

I brought my car to a stop, backed up just a little, and then pulled off to the side of the road. I scanned the woods with my binoculars and found that there was indeed a small pond hidden among the trees. Shielded from the road by a hedge of honeysuckle and raspberry bushes during the summer, the pond was impossible to see until the leaves dropped and let the secret out. Still, even then I managed to drive by this spot many times without noticing there was water just a little ways off the road.

There was still ice on the water, covering perhaps one third of the pond's surface area, and the rest of the pond was mostly water. The rain was gentle enough that I could see the individual halos of expanding waves sent out by the raindrops. Near the edge of the ice the halos slowed, interfered with by little slushy icebergs that had broken free. No Titanic would ply these waters, so the little bergs offered nothing more than accent to the scene; winter was losing its grip, but very slowly.

I was almost ready to put the car in gear and resume my search when a slight movement caught my eye. It took me a minute to figure out what it was I was looking at, but all of a sudden I realized that the little pond was serving as refuge and rest stop for a pair of hooded mergansers. Both birds were snoozing with bills snugly tucked under wings and both were ever so slowly drifting through the slushy margins of the water where it met the ice. Perhaps my notion that no Titanics plied these waters was a bit premature, though they certainly seemed in no danger of sinking.

I lowered the passenger side window and rested my lens on the door. I knew that there was absolutely no way I could get out of the car without scaring the mergansers, so I did my best to find a clear spot through the naked branches between me and my subjects before I snapped a photo. The end effect was one of very soft focus and the picture managed to capture the dark, introspective quality of the day. I visited the same little pond every day for the following week, but never saw the mergansers there again. I guess I just got lucky.

After taking the pictures of the mergansers I decided that it was time to continue. I put the car in gear, slowly moved off the snowy margin, and decided it was time to look for open water.

This turned out to be much easier than I had expected because the temperatures had been relatively steady and warm for a few weeks and all of the local lakes were at least partially free of ice. In less than twenty minutes I found myself parked beside an extensive body of water known as the Watervliet Reservoir. The water in this impoundment is always somewhat murky, but it is a magnet for waterfowl in the springtime. I was sure that there would be something worth seeing there that day, but I had no idea that I would be making my inaugural annual visit to this site to observe ring-necked ducks.

It took me about two seconds to realize that I was seeing something for the first time. These birds were vaguely familiar looking, but there was something that just didn't seem to add up. They clearly weren't buffleheads or goldeneyes, but they did look quite a bit like scaups. I supposed scaups were possible at that time of year, but there was just something about that identification that still didn't sit right. Rather than get too carried away with what the ducks were, however, I decided to focus my attention on taking photographs and worry about identifying them at a later time. I took several rolls of pictures that first day, and in subsequent years I have returned to the same spot and taken hundreds of digital photos. It's always amazing how a once unknown species of wildlife can become a regular and routine part of anyone's wildlife observations once you know when and where to look for it.

That first encounter with the ducks will always be special. I spent more than two hours sitting in a parked car in the rain with no engine running. When there were no cars in close proximity on the highway that runs past the reservoir, I could hear that light hissing sound of a gentle rain falling into water that so very closely resembles the sound of bacon frying in a pan. In addition to the ring-necked ducks I also saw mallards, common mergansers, Canada geese, and even a few northern pintails way off in the distance. When it was finally time to go, I turned the engine over, put the jeep in gear, and made my way home through the back roads to the comforting rhythm of the wipers.

Killdeer

About a mile down the road from my house there is a field that is absolutely ideal for killdeer. It is an almost perfect 10-acre square with grasses growing in a mixture of gravel and thin topsoil, which means the grasses that add their green shoots to the landscape don't grow particularly tall or thick.

Additionally, this field is bordered on all sides by paved roads. Each of these roads has wide margins lined with coarse stone fill. The town has even abandoned one of these roads, and vehicles seldom use it. As a result, it offers the wide-open spaces that killdeer prefer with none of the hazards associated with heavy traffic.

This is all fine and dandy, but one other random modification has opened up this field to me as a photographer. Last year, on the opposite side of the abandoned road, a restaurant was opened. The grand opening was celebrated with a massive party, and the owners apparently needed some extra parking, so a gravel horseshoe road was put out into the middle of the field. This had two positive effects.

First, the gravel is a fantastic surface for me to drive on, which means that I can easily get into the middle of the field with my Jeep. Second, and more importantly, the presence of gravel has made the field even more attractive to killdeer as potential nesting substrate. Things just seem to be getting better and better for the killdeer in this particular spot.

So every year I simply have to wait for the killdeer to arrive and, as so many things in Nature seem to be, this is always predictable and surprising at the same time. Typically, killdeer arrive in March. This always seems far too early, yet it happens again and again, year after year. If I'm out on a nature photography jaunt, I'll take a little extra time on the way home and see if the field has any new visitors.

Sometimes there is still snow on the ground, which is not uncommon for killdeer to have to contend with, but it always strikes me as being a little odd nonetheless. The killdeer, after all, is a member of the plover family, which would look much

Killdeer will feign injury to lure predators away from a nest.

more at home on the beaches and rocky coasts along the ocean. But instead of patrolling the shallows of some coastal bay, this bird can often be seen standing on a pile of icy snow and picking for worms in the soggy soil.

These early encounters with killdeer are a great treat, but from a photographer's point of view they often leave a lot to be desired. For one thing, I am usually unprepared for a killdeer-stalking session, which means I usually don't have my big lens with me. I usually manage to capture some pretty startling images of killdeer in snow, but I know that a little planning will always make my second killdeer encounter of any given year much more productive.

So the following weekend I'll get up early and head straight to the field. It usually takes all of thirty seconds to find the birds, and sometimes I'm rewarded for my efforts by finding not just one pair, but two. This is always great because I am able to listen

The killdeer is a member of the plover family.

to these birds fight over ownership of their new territories. How the field will be divided is still unknown, but the antics of the birds are a riot.

There is always a great deal of posing and posturing going on, and all the while the birds make their high-pitched call notes. Then there will inevitably be some running and chasing. This can go on and on, back and forth, and I'm not sure if anything is really ever settled.

I do know, however, that in addition to being greatly entertained I can also become quite frustrated. Sometimes the birds will stay just a little too far out of range for my liking. Even if I have my big lens, I am always amazed how close you have to be to get the great frame-filling shots that show all of the details you want to see. I keep pleading with the birds to wander closer to my car, but sometimes they just won't do it.

You see, a car is as good as a photography blind because most animals don't seem to realize that there is a person inside it. As long as the car is relatively quiet, and slow, you can do pretty well. But if I were to open the door and put a foot on the ground, the story would be quite different. Suddenly, a human has appeared, and all interesting behavior stops and is replaced with high-alert, ready-to-fly behavior.

Well, as I sit there cursing their reluctance to get any closer than sixty feet, I know it is just a matter of time until I get the chance I am waiting for. Instead of moving parallel to the car, a bird will turn straight toward me, possibly even being followed by others. This is the reward for my patience.

But isn't it funny how sometimes you can get too much of something you wish for? Sometimes the birds never stop moving. My 800-mm lens is great over longer distances, but it has such a narrow field of view that locking onto a moving target can be quite a challenge. Add to that the fact that it is just so heavy, and I sometimes have a big problem. If the birds walk within twelve feet of my position, I may never be able to lock onto them if they never stop moving. That faint scream you heard off in the distance on Saturday . . . that was me.

But I never give up. After about an hour I can be fairly certain that the birds will become acclimated to the presence of my Jeep, and that is when they will start to ignore me. They may even move onto a slope by the side of one of the roads, into ideal position for me to photograph them with the sun at my back. One year, after a particularly long test of my patience, I got some of the best killdeer photos I have ever taken.

So here is where my long-term project begins. Once the birds have established themselves, I simply have to make regular visits to the field in an attempt to keep them accustomed to seeing me. This way they will feel more comfortable when I am around, and they will display all of their normal behavior while I capture it on film. Long-term observation might even allow me to locate nests, and this in turn could lead to my ultimate goal of photographing killdeer chicks.

The world is filled with many beautiful creatures, but few could be more adorable than baby plovers. Imagine baby chickens—fluffy balls of down with little heads, big eyes, and big legs. Now add to this the fact that the legs are a little longer and they are toddling around in the open grass with their parents. I swear Walt Disney himself had a hand in designing these little creatures!

Killdeer lay their eggs directly on the ground.

Wildflowers

I thought I might take the liberty of creating a day of flower finding for you. Pretend it's a Sunday morning and it's 5:30 a.m. You awake refreshed and well rested and you realize it's your day off. The sun is shining, you hop out of bed, throw on some old jeans, grab a quick cup of coffee, and in just seven minutes you're ready to . . . Wait a minute, wait a minute, hold on, WHOAH! For a minute there I forgot that I was writing a flower-watching story and I started writing the introduction to a bird-watching story. Don't panic, there's no need to get up this early, or even do anything out of the ordinary on this particular morning. So go back to bed, get a little more sleep, and let me start again.

It's Sunday morning and it's . . . 8:30 a.m. You awake refreshed and well rested and you realize it's your day off. You ease yourself out of bed, slip on some old . . . slippers, grab a cup of coffee that a loved one has made especially for you, and in just . . . twenty minutes you're ready to . . . go get the morning paper. The sun is shining, the air is fresh, and as you walk down the driveway, you notice a couple of spots of color in the lawn. The dandelions are easy to spot. Normally you would make a mental note that you need to find a way to get rid of them, but that surprise cup of Java has you in a really good mood. So instead of cursing them, you bend down to look at one. It actually is a very beautiful flower, isn't it? As you look closer, you notice that the dandelion flower isn't just one flower, but a collection of many tiny flowers in an "inflorescence." Then you recall something you learned about flowers in junior high. What was that word again? Something like *stanems, stymes,* or *stamens*? Stamens, that's right. Didn't they have something to do with guns?

You take a sip of coffee, sit down in the grass, close your eyes, and begin to remember. A flower generally has four main parts. The sepals are what cover the flower when it is still in the bud stage. As soon as the flower blooms, they tend to just curl up and roll out of the way. The petals are usually bright colors, and they are designed to give birds and insects a bright target. Then you get to the important parts—the stamens and pistils. The stamens are the male parts of the flowers and are composed of a long filament with an anther at the top. The anther is where the pollen is produced, and each grain of pollen contains sperm cells. The filament holds the anthers up so the pollen can be out in the open. The pistils (not pistols) are the female portions of flowers. Each is composed of ovaries, a style, and a stigma. The ovaries hold the egg cells, the style is basically the same as

Marsh marigold.

a filament, and the stigma rests upon the top of the style and has a sticky surface to capture pollen. You smile to yourself and think that there is no reason to attach a stigma to a bad-smelling flower because it still has style. Yikes, what's in that coffee you're drinking?

Shaken from your memories, you pop your eyes open, get up and take a quick look around to make sure no one saw you taking your trip down memory lane. You head for the mailbox, but before you get that far, you notice some other flowers in the lawn. There are blue and white violets—those are pretty easy—but there is another one you aren't too sure about. You collect the paper, pick one of these mystery flowers, and head back to the kitchen. Once inside, you retrieve your flower guide (everyone should have one) and you start the process of identification. Hmmm . . . it has purple flowers, the main stem is square instead of round, and the leaves are very small with scalloped edges. The book says it is a flower called Jill-over-the-ground, and it is very pretty but, ah, it's an alien. You want to find some native wildflowers.

A quick family meeting and it is decided a walk in the woods is in order. A quick drive and you're there (wherever there may be), on the trail and eyes at the ready. If you walk past a swampy spot, you will likely catch sight of some beautiful plants covered with bright yellow flowers. These usually grow in shallow running water, and they look like potted plants that have been set into a stream. These are marsh marigolds. Also known as cowslip, this flower belongs to the buttercup family. This is another of the showiest and most attractive wildflowers in our area, and it can often be seen from your car as you drive past marshy areas.

As you continue walking, you come upon some odd-looking red and yellow flowers in a rocky area. The flowers 'look' down at the ground and appear to be composed of tubular red petals with very long pistils and stamens. A quick look in your flower book confirms your suspicions—this is wild columbine. A particular favorite of ruby-throated hummingbirds, this is a nectar-producing flower that also attracts many species of butterflies. Then you come upon two very odd-looking plants by the side of a field. One is not even green, but rather a pinkish tan. It has what appears to be a cone-shaped . . . thing . . . at the top of the stem. It actually reminds you of asparagus. Look as you may, however, you cannot find it in your flower book. Well, don't worry, it isn't in any of my flower books either because it isn't a flower. To find this one you would need to get a book on ferns for you have found yourself a field horsetail. It is the most common of the many species of horsetails, and it can be found growing in almost any soil. The plants will grow on the sides of railroad tracks, on slag heaps and vacant lots, but you can also find them in fields and wooded areas that get some sunlight. They are peculiar, but still rather beautiful, so I thought you might like to know what they are.

Another beautiful flower is the trout lily. This is an easy one to identify because the leaves grow directly out of the ground and are green mottled with brown. The six petals of this species are a beautiful yellow, and this flower too 'looks' down at the ground. Fortunately, the entire plant stands about 10 inches off the ground, so if you are gentle, you can bend the flower upward for a better look at it.

The farther you walk, and the more often you walk, the more you will see. There are hundreds of flowers that bloom in the spring, and every day there will be something new. There are wild bleeding hearts, Dutchman's breeches, May apples, hawkweed, devil's bit, and even a tall flowering shrub called pinxter flower. Be careful though, because they won't last forever. A virtual flower walk is a beautiful thing because it can fuel the imagination and provide inspiration on a cold and rainy . . . even snowy . . . day. Nothing, however, can take the place of a real walk in real woods to see the real flowers.

Bird Songs

Every year there is a fairly dependable sign that the transition between winter and spring has actually taken place. It's not a subtle sign either. You don't have to examine tree buds with magnifying lenses, or even know any equations for calculating heating-degree-days. All you need to do is step outside . . . and listen.

Even before the grass starts greening, or the earliest flowers start blooming, there is a change in sound. The transition from winter to spring is a transition from quiet to raucous, contemplative to boisterous, and we owe it all to birds.

But did you ever wonder why birds sing? Why do they spend such an enormous part of their lives making such an enormous amount of noise? Many have asked this question, some have tried to uncover the answer, and this is what we have discovered:

First and foremost, animals make sounds because they need to communicate. Squirrels chatter, mice squeak, and foxes bark because they are trying to tell other squirrels, mice, or foxes what is going on in their lives. This does not explain song, however, for with very few exceptions, mammals do not sing. But why?

Mammals are highly skilled at communicating through the use of chemicals. Anyone who has a dog or a cat will notice that these mammals spend a lot of time sniffing things. Basically, they are taking chemical samples of their surroundings in an effort to figure out what's going on in the neighborhood.

Since mammals are such experts when it comes to this chemical communication, they don't need to use their voices. Most birds, on the other hand, don't have much of a sense of smell, so they have to come up with something else.

Now this would certainly explain why birds might turn to vocal communication, but it doesn't necessarily explain bird song. For instance, the need for communication and the inability to communicate through a sense of smell should affect all birds in the same way. But not all birds sing. If you think about it, you will realize that big birds tend to be fairly quiet, while the smaller birds are the ones that make a lot of noise.

This is partly because big birds are easy to see, and partly because big birds tend to be found in areas where their size does not interfere with their movements (that is, open places where

A male song sparrow throws his head back in song.

they are even easier to see). The birds that do a lot of singing tend to be smaller and to live in habitats full of trees, bushes, and grasses, which make it difficult to see.

Anyone who has gone camping in a forest with a bunch of children can certainly attest to the fact that once they get out among the trees, they start yelling. They are doing this so that they can keep track of one another's whereabouts. The more frequently they move, the more frequently they need to confirm their position relative to the group, and the so they yell more, and more, and more. It is usually at this point that the adults in the group reach for the aspirin.

Birds do the same thing. Most birds have nonmusical contact notes that they utilize for the purpose of keeping track of one another, just like kids on a camping trip in the woods. Yet I am sure that all of you will agree that yelling and singing are two very different things. Small size, complex habitats, and the need to communicate (but being unable to communicate through smell) still don't explain song.

Well, it turns out that male birds do the majority of singing, so it stands to reason that they have some important things they need to say. Male birds need to identify themselves. They need everyone else to know who they are, how old they are, how attached they are, and, most significantly, where they live. Singing is all about territory.

Imagine that you are a small bird and you live in a forest. It's springtime and you want to have babies. To support a mate, and the family she will provide for you, you need to have a territory full of food and good nesting areas. You have to advertise yourself, and you have to use sound to do it. The problem is that all of the other male birds are thinking the same thing, so you can't use simple sounds.

There are hundreds of other birds that might live in your forest, so you have to use a pattern of sounds that is unique to your species. As a result, you cannot use the universal sounds for "Danger" that all birds appear to understand. Your sounds have to be complex—they have to be songs.

Songs serve as a stern warning to other males and a reassuring invitation to females. Frequent and energetic songs may be an advertisement that the singer is still unattached, while less frequent, more relaxed songs indicate contentment. Many males continue to sing so that other males of the same species know that they are still occupying a territory.

In other cases, male birds sing so that their offspring can learn their songs. Baby birds don't have a lot to do while they are sitting in their nests, but the babies of some species are learning. Young females are learning the songs of their fathers so they know what to listen for when they look for mates of their own. Young males are learning the songs so they can grow up to sing them properly.

In fact, young male birds that have to learn their songs actually spend quite a bit of time singing quietly to themselves. They listen to their fathers, and then try to sing the same kind of song, but not too loudly. They certainly don't want to get into an argument with an adult male, but I imagine that they don't want to be embarrassed either.

Finally, there is one last element to bird song that I find particularly appealing. I get the feeling that some birds sing because they enjoy it. This is not a novel idea, either. In 1973, Charles Hartshorne, a professor of philosophy at the University of Texas, Austin, published a book in which he wrote: "Birds and other animals sing and thereby win and keep a mate and, in many cases, also territories; but the energetic persistence in singing may be sustained partly by a feeling, however primitive, for the beauty of the sounds they are making." I think this is a marvelous idea.

The sounds of March are like the raindrops of an approaching storm. The first new sound is always a surprise, like a stray raindrop hitting your face, and it is usually made by a red-winged blackbird. The traditional April showers which bring May flowers do so by providing rain on the landscape, but April also brings showers of song. More and more birds arrive, singing more and more songs, until May blooms with a profusion of sounds that are as bright and cheerful as any wildflowers.

If ever you find yourself with a free moment, particularly in the morning, I would definitely suggest that you go outside and enjoy the songs of the birds in your neighborhood. You don't even have to know who is singing which song to enjoy the concert. All you need to do is open your mind to the possibility that the birds are excited, happy, and looking forward to a wonderful year. Maybe a little bit of their optimism even will rub off on you, and you can carry it with you wherever you have to go that day.

A male eastern towhee.

The Eastern Bluebird

Though it is hard to imagine now, there was once a time in my life when I had never seen a bluebird. Sure, I had heard of them, who hadn't? They were the "Bluebirds of Happiness," and there was that song "Zip-A-Dee-Doo-Dah" with the line "Mr. Bluebird on my shoulder. . . ." They were out there somewhere, but they were hardly ever seen, and until I finally saw one I had no idea what I was missing.

Humans may hold the title of the most intelligent species on the planet, but being intelligent does not automatically mean that we are smart. Our actions can be so blindly and poorly planned that we can never hope to fully appreciate the events we set into motion. We always know when we have made a mistake, however, for it is at these times that we risk losing the things that we hold most dear. This was true in the case of the eastern bluebird, for there was actually a time when it was almost lost to us all.

When European colonists first came to North America, they found vast and beautiful forests . . . forests that they immediately cut down to make room for farming. By changing the habitat, they started to favor certain birds, and the bluebird was one of them. Bluebirds nested in old woodpecker holes and other natural cavities in trees, but they had a particular fondness for grassy areas where they could hunt for insects. The pesticide-free fields of the early farmers must have been perfect for them.

The farmers surely got to know these delightful little birds, and believe me, once you know them, you cannot help but fall in love with them. They have certain qualities that simply reach out to your heart. For instance, when a male is sitting on a perch and catches sight of his mate, he will gently flap one wing, as though he were waving hello to her. If the male approaches the female, then she will wave her wing at him. This is the way blue-birds greet one another, and it is one of the most touching rituals I have ever seen animals perform. As you shall see, it holds a special meaning to me.

Eastern bluebird.

Eventually, the farming activities that had initially favored bluebirds began to harm them. In 1850 the house sparrow was introduced in Brooklyn, New York, in the hope that it would help to control agricultural insect pests. Unfortunately, house sparrows were also very aggressive cavity nesters that could easily push bluebirds out of their homes. Without thinking about it, we had introduced a mortal enemy of our beloved "Bluebird of Happiness," and in only fifty years the house sparrow had colonized the entire country. Quite a strange way to show our appreciation for a beloved friend.

Fortunately, this introduction coincided with the discovery of gold in California, the opening of the Erie Canal, and the completion of the transcontinental railroad. Humans began to abandon the eastern United States, and this may have softened the blow that we never intended to deliver. House sparrows may be vicious competitors of the bluebird, but they were also strongly dependent on humans for food. So as the fields began to grow in, the bluebirds could head for the country while the sparrows stayed close to the towns.

This worked for about forty years, until our forefathers blundered again. In 1890 a new bird was introduced to North America—the European starling. Fans of Shakespeare thought it would be wonderful to bring all of the birds mentioned in his plays to the New World, and the United States Acclimatization Society released sixty starlings in Central Park. The avian and human inhabitants of North America have suffered ever since.

The European starling is another cavity nester that went after bluebirds, woodpeckers, and even house sparrows. Starlings are much larger than house sparrows, and their tenacity allows them to evict even the relatively large northern flicker (a woodpecker) from nest cavities. Unlike the house sparrow, however, the starling quickly became a serious problem for farmers. Starlings were eating so much grain and cattle feed that in 1960 a California project resulted in the slaughter of 9 million of them. Despite this kind of pressure, the starling is ubiquitous throughout the United States today.

The combined effects of the house sparrow and the European starling might have spelled the end for the bluebird if not for the efforts of Dr. T. E. Musselman of Quincy, Illinois. Bluebirds had completely disappeared from his part of the country, and he was determined to bring them back. It was clear that bluebirds were suffering from a lack of nesting sites out in the country where they could escape the pressures of their new enemies.

Eastern bluebird.

So Dr. Musselman decided to create nest cavities for them by building nest boxes. In 1933 he put out twenty-two boxes along a country road and created the first "bluebird trail." In following years he added more and more nest boxes until in 1935 he had placed 102 boxes along 43 miles of country roads, 86 percent of which were occupied by bluebirds. In that same year he wrote a report in which he stated, "For the first time in twenty years bluebirds are a common sight along the roads of Adams County, Illinois, and I believe that any other enthusiast can duplicate this." He was right!

The idea caught on, and people everywhere were putting up bluebird trails. Today, bluebirds are once again a common sight throughout their range. They are still vulnerable to attacks by house sparrows, but they have other allies in their fight for survival—tree swallows.

Bluebirds and tree swallows have a very special relationship. Both birds are very territorial and refuse to tolerate others of their own kind in close proximity to their nests. For some reason, however, they do not seem to object to each other all that much. This means that you can place two nest boxes about fifteen feet apart, and instead of fighting, they make good neighbors. A solitary box may be fought over, but two boxes alleviate all conflicts other than an initial squabble over who gets which box.

Once the selection is made, both pairs will defend their overlapping territories from house sparrows and starlings. This cooperation exists probably because the two birds occupy such different ecological niches. Tree swallows are aerial hunters, while bluebirds spend most of their time hunting on the ground. The only thing they share in common is their choice of nesting sites, but as long as there are enough nest boxes, there are no problems.

In the spring of 1991 my life took a turn for the better when I had my very first experience with nesting bluebirds. I lived in a house in Montague, Massachusetts, and this house sat on the edge of a big, grassy field. I put up a nest box in the hope that a pair of these little blue angels might appear from nowhere, but I had no idea that it would work so well, or so quickly. I had seen bluebirds before, but only from a great distance. Nothing could have prepared me for the treat of seeing a pair of them up close.

Yet two days later, there they were, examining the box I had offered up. The female quickly decided that this would be a good place to raise a family, and in just two days she built a nest of fine, soft grasses. It took her five days to lay a clutch of five blue eggs, and in two weeks she had five little babies. All the while the male could be heard singing to her, and since bluebirds are members of the thrush family, they have great little songs. When he sang, you would have thought he was the king of the world.

Unfortunately, I did not know of the dangers of house sparrows, and tragedy struck. A local pair of house sparrows appeared from nowhere and killed all but one of the babies. The survivor was a male, and although he did live, he had lost his right eye. As a graduate student studying wildlife biology, I quickly realized that he was not releasable, so he was raised to 'like' humans, which I think every bluebird does anyway. During his first spring he grew the most magnificent blue feathers on his head, back and wings, his breast turned orange like a robin's, and he began to sing. He even waved his wings at me whenever he saw me.

I lived with him for four years, and I have memories of him I will always cherish. Perhaps the most special memories are of those times when he would fly down to sit on my shoulder and offer me a bug, sing quietly in my ear, or simply sit with me while he preened his feathers. He truly was the "Bluebird of Happiness," and he opened my eyes to the rich and wonderfully personal lives of birds.

Trilliums

Mid-spring has its own wonderful feeling! The nights remain cool, and the days can be a mixture of cool, warm, and almost hot. There are periods of dry sunshine followed by long rains, and it all adds up to a great time for wildflowers.

Now there are beautiful flowers of all shapes and sizes out there, but certain species have that perfect combination of color and form which makes them classics. When it comes to elegance and popularity, I can think of few flowers that can match the wild trilliums. If you want to see your local trilliums without having to brave your local blackflies, early May is the time to start looking!

Members of the lily family, trilliums are plants that have designed their lives on a principle of threes. The plants have three symmetrical leaves that grow on a single, thin stem. The developing blossoms are protected by three fleshy *sepals*, which form the bud when the flower is closed, and serve to elegantly balance the petals of the flower when the blossom finally opens.

The bisexual flowers (i.e., flowers that have both male and female structures present) have six pollen-producing anthers (a multiple of three) and three pistils which lead to the ovary (also in three sections.) When it comes to sticking to a family plan, trilliums are fanatics.

There are about ten species of trilliums that can be found in the eastern United States, but in the Northeast there are only two that I would classify as being really common. The first of these is the red trillium.

The elegant flower of this plant, also known by the names *purple trillium, wake robin,* and *birthroot,* is a deep maroon color and is beautifully complemented by the lush green leaves. The plant can grow to over 18 inches in height, and the flower is on a 2- to 4-inch stem that droops slightly. As a result, you usually have to get down on your knees to get a really good look at one.

As beautiful as the flower looks, however, I would not take a strong sniff of a red trillium flower. Simply put, these flowers STINK! But why would a flower stink? There is always an interesting reason for such things, and I am happy to say that we are not to be disappointed with the red trillium.

Red trillium.

Like many flowers, the red trillium depends on insects for pollination. Flowers that rely on bees and butterflies for pollination attract them with sweet perfumes because that is what the bees and butterflies like.

But red trilliums are a little different. Instead of bees and butterflies, red trillium flowers rely on flies as pollinators. Specifically, they rely on carrion flies, and there is no better way to attract a carrion fly than with the smell of rotting meat. Hence, these beautiful flowers smell awful.

Now as unpleasant as this may seem, it did give rise to a rather curious human behavior not too long ago. Back in the good old days, physicians of European descent had the custom of using plants as medicines to treat afflictions that the plants resembled in some respect. As a result, the fetid red trillium was used to treat gangrene.

A tea made from the root of the plant was used to treat asthma, difficult breathing, and various lung disorders. With the aid of modern technology, we now know that the root of the red trillium has a rich supply of steroids. This most certainly played a role in its effectiveness for respiratory disorders.

Native Americans also used the red trillium as a medicine. The origin of the name *birthroot* undoubtedly lies in the custom of using the plant to treat a variety of stages of the female reproductive cycle. To aid in conception, the root of the plant was used as an aphrodisiac, and after conception the plant was used to help induce childbirth and to aid in labor. Later in life it was also used to treat menstrual disorders and menopause.

Red trilliums are abundant in our area and bloom from April to June. I have noticed, however, that they tend to fade out by the end of May. I have found them to be particularly numerous up in the hill towns surrounding my home, and at those higher altitudes it may still be possible to find fresh flowers still in full bloom in the later part of the flowering season. Look for them along trails and dirt roads through rich deciduous forests.

The second common trillium in our area, the painted trillium, is arguably one of the most beautiful of all of our native wildflowers. Typically much smaller than its red cousin, the painted trillium plants I have seen are usually somewhere between 6 and 12 inches tall, and the leaves are smaller, more brown in color, and less lush.

The flowers too are usually smaller than those of the red trillium, but they make up for their small size with color! Each of the three white petals has a V-shaped patch of bright pink. In addition to the bright color, the flowers are on a much shorter stem than those of the red trillium, and they grow facing the sky. No need to get down on your hands and knees to enjoy these flowers.

Oddly enough there is no mention of any medicinal uses for the painted trillium. Neither is there any mention of their having an offensive odor. Now the lack of any similarity to gangrene might play a role here, but I suspect that there is an even simpler explanation.

Painted trillium.

Red and painted trilliums have a very similar distribution. The red trillium can be found from Ontario east to Nova Scotia and south through Michigan and New England to Delaware and West Virginia. From there it sticks to the mountains and spreads south to Georgia and west to Tennessee.

The painted trillium can be found in basically the same range, but is found a little further west into Manitoba and Wisconsin. It is also absent from Delaware. Yet even though the ranges of the two plants are similar, painted trilliums are not as abundant as red trilliums.

So it could be that painted trilliums have properties similar to those of their larger red cousins, but are small enough and rare enough to make harvesting them seem a little silly. Why look for the small bottle of medicine when you can find the big one nearby, right?

If you go in search of painted trilliums, you will still want to look in rich, moist forests, but you will also want to find slightly acidic conditions. Basically, this means you will want to find a forest that has either a lot of oaks or a lot of pine trees and other conifers.

Both of these beautiful flowers bloom from April into June, but painted trilliums bloom more abundantly in the latter portion of the season. As I mentioned earlier, the flowers in higher elevations will probably be more vibrant.

Fortunately, the flower on each plant will last for about two weeks. So if you should happen to find a particularly nice patch of either variety, you will have time to go get a friend and share. Just remember that there is no better medicine for a gloomy day than spending time with a friend and looking for wildflowers.

Baby Time

During a very special Memorial Day weekend just a few years ago, I witnessed two events that bring a smile to my face even now. Both of these events involved the wondrous appearance of new little lives in the fields around my home. Both of these events were things that I predict every year but could never have actually expected in a million years. Your close attention will help you to understand what I mean.

One fine Saturday, just about noon, my lovely wife and I set off from the house to do a little grocery shopping. On our way to town we passed through some beautiful rural country dominated by a smattering of early-regeneration forest, large, luxurious hay fields, and mature woods. I have no recollection of what we were talking about, but I do remember my voice trailing off to nothing as we turned a certain corner.

I immediately started to scan the fields for something out of place . . . as I always do. Basically, I was looking for turkeys or deer. I always suspect that I will see something if only I look closely enough, and on that particular day there was a deer standing right out in the middle of that hayfield! Suspicion confirmed . . . behavior reinforced.

Two, possibly three seconds after spotting the deer, however, I noticed that something was a bit off. The deer seemed 'too thick' in the region of her hindquarters. The spark of a remote possibility appeared somewhere in the back of my mind, but I knew it was impossible . . . at least a week too early for such a thing to occur. As the distance between my car and the deer closed, however, possibility very quickly became reality.

It wasn't just a doe standing in the field. It was a doe and her newborn fawn! I gently brought the car to a halt (didn't want to scare the family) and watched for all of thirty seconds. The doe was on high alert, and she spent most of her time licking her baby. The fawn, ridiculously small and still a little wobbly, spent most of its time nursing. I was elated and horrified all at once.

The owner of the field was out in his yard mowing the grass. He was probably 300 yards from where my car sat, and I cannot be sure if he ever looked up to see what I was up to, but I am certain that he had no clue that a fawn had been born in his hay. Thank Darwin's beard that he wasn't walking his dogs at that particular moment!

I looked at Susan. She said, "You've got to." So I made an immediate U-turn and raced back to the house. Never, never go anywhere without a camera!! It took me four to five minutes to get back to the house, grab camera and film, and race back to the scene. Anything could have happened in that time, but I had to try. As it turned out, there was another vehicle just in front of me on the way back, and the driver of that vehicle was a fellow scanner. As we approached the turn, the brake lights came on, and there were now two of us stopped by the roadside.

A doe leads her newborn fawn to safety.

Well, that was all the doe could stand. I am sure she would have bounded off if not for the simple fact that she had a newborn in tow. Instead, she made a measured retreat and had to stop every ten yards or so to allow her wobbly little baby to catch up. I recorded most of the retreat on film, and when I reviewed the photos, I was impressed that the first frame was clearly the best.

It didn't take long for the doe to make it to the woods. By that time the other driver had become uninterested and had moved on, which allowed Susan and me to move up and get a

Young fawns will curl up and remain still in an effort to stay safe.

better angle. The doe kept looking back at us while she waited for the fawn to catch up to her, and then they both slipped into the safety of the trees. That marked the magical end of sighting number one.

Sighting number two, which occurred the following day, was just as interesting but much easier for me to observe. It was Sunday morning, and Susan and I were enjoying a little breakfast at the kitchen table. The big windows that look out over our backyard allow us to monitor the comings and goings of the various birds that visit our feeders, and this time it was Susan who picked up on something.

An immature bluebird sits in my lawn after it fledges.

"Why is the bluebird chasing that big black bird?" she said. I glanced out the window and saw that there was indeed a black bird out by one of the bluebird boxes, but seeing as it was a grackle, I started to form a comment that focused on the proper use of the adjective *big*. Crows are 'big,' while grackles are merely 'bigger.' You know . . . something idiotic like that.

Before the words could escape my mouth, however, my mind fixated on the behavior of the birds and came to another conclusion. "Yeah, I wonder what's up?" is all I said as I put down my coffee and headed out the door. I had a feeling I knew what was up!

In less than a minute I had walked to the nest box and found two baby bluebirds sitting on the lawn with the vacant expressions of pure oblivion glued to their little faces. One was preening its feathers while the other was looking around. Both had been noticed by some of the neighbors. Again, thank Darwin's beard that they hadn't been noticed by the big black birds!

I moved the babies to a nearby hedge of honeysuckles and raced back to get my camera. Never go anywhere without a camera!! I raced back down, took a couple of quick pictures, and then retreated to the house again to monitor things from a safe distance. How was the male bluebird going to look after two fledglings out of the nest while also feeding the two (I checked) that remained in the box? How was the doe going to keep that tiny little fawn alive?

The next day, a Monday, was when I noticed a tractor parked in the corner of the hayfield where I had seen the fawn. The time for mowing the first hay had arrived, but what if that field wasn't empty? What if it was a nursery? I had also seen dogs running loose in the neighborhood, and just a few days before the bluebirds fledged I chased a cat out of my yard. Dogs, cats, and mowers could have brought these stories to horrifying ends!

The end of May is the beginning of "baby time," and we should all try to keep that in mind as we go about our business. It is a wonder that any of these little creatures survive more than a day out in the wild, but it is a certainty that many do not. It is a big, dangerous world out there. Coyotes, hawks, crows and weasels are all bad enough, but cats, dogs, mowers and cars are unnecessary factors of mortality for baby animals.

So slow down, keep your dogs on leashes, and keep your cats inside for a while. Why not give all of the newest members of our wild neighborhood a chance to grow up safely?

A baby common yellowthroat sits in safety.

SUMMER

American Ceasar's mushroom.

Marvelous Mushrooms

Like all of the seasons, summer has many feels and flavors to it. There are those wonderful first days in June when the days are so long, and the Fourth of July is just around the corner. There are the sweltering "dog days" of August, when the Earth seems bent upon the solitary goal of roasting you alive, and then there are those days in mid-September, still technically summer, when the heat is finally turned off and the bugs start to die down.

As a youngster, I think I was always aware of these changes, but was never able to really describe what was happening because I simply didn't understand enough about the world. All I could really understand (like many kids who grow up outdoors) were the "lazy" days of summer. These were the days spent floating on an inner tube in the middle of a pond, or chasing the creatures that lived in the shallow margins of the pond.

But what I really looked forward to most was Labor Day. To me this was the day of days (almost better than Christmas) because it meant my family would once again make its long, ancestral journey to the Adirondacks, where we would spend a week reveling in 2,800 acres of nature's perfection known as Camp Little Notch.

We abandoned TV, newspapers, and anything else to do with the outside world, and we lost ourselves in a crystal-clear lake, the tall hemlocks, the long forest streams, and the dark, starlit nights. It was a magical time and one that still resonates in every member of my family. I think it is the children, however, who were able to make the most of it.

We were not responsible for anything, so we were allowed to play. When we were at home, we always had to let my mother know where we were going, how we were getting there, whom we were going with, and when we would be back. At camp, however, we could disappear for hours on end without worrying my mother in the slightest. We were in the middle of nowhere, with no one else around, and my parents were at ease.

For these wonderful forays, my grandmother always gave us a standing order: be on the lookout for mushrooms. My mother was an artist of some acclaim, and she was always encouraging my brother and sister and me to draw frogs, snails, and mushrooms. Granny, on the other hand, seemed to know much more about all of them. She knew their names, and she knew their secrets.

She also needed as many examples of mushrooms as she could get her hands on because, as the camp's naturalist, she

Yellow pholiota.

liked to open up the nature center and offer classes to the other campers. One of her favorite projects, and I must admit it was one of my favorites as well, was making mushroom spore prints. Like all organisms on Earth, mushrooms have a life cycle that they must adhere to. The cycle is easy enough to understand, but as with any cycle there is always the challenge of where to begin. I have struggled with this for years and have finally settled on a starting point that makes the most sense for mushrooms—the spore.

A fungal spore is a haploid cell, which means that it has only half the normal number of chromosomes. Both animals and plants utilize a similar system for their reproduction in the sense that both groups manufacture egg and sperm cells. The really big difference with fungal spores, however, is the fact that the spores can live quite nicely on their own.

Spores are finer than talcum powder and are easily carried on even the most subtle of breezes. At this very moment a thin atmosphere of fungal spores surrounds each of us. They settle on our skin and clothes, and we even inhale them. The key to the survival of the spores is their random arrival in a suitable place to live. The vast majority of fungal spores never make it.

For the most part, the types of fungi that we call "mushrooms" are heterotrophic decomposers. In terms easier to understand, mushrooms are organisms that cannot make their own food. Instead, they must ingest pre-existing organic molecules, and they obtain these molecules by 'eating' dead organisms.

So your typical fungal spore, floating on the winds of chance, hopes to land in a cool, damp place where a lot of dead organic matter can be found. In other words, it's hoping to land on the forest floor, or someplace with similar properties. Once this happens, the spore will 'hatch' and start to grow, much in the same way that a seed germinates.

A solitary fungal filament called a *hypha* will emerge from the spore capsule and begin the process of 'eating.' To do this, the cells of the hypha excrete digestive enzymes that break down organic molecules into smaller pieces and then (for lack of a better way of putting it) they "slurp up" the molecules they need.

Humans have stomachs that we use to digest our food internally, but mushrooms do all of their digesting outside their bodies. As time passes, the single hypha will branch out and expand into many *hyphae* (pronounced HIGH-fee), which closely resemble the root system of a plant. Once you get a large enough mass of hyphae in one place, you have what is known as a *primary mycelium* (pronounced migh-SEE-lee-uhm). The fungus can survive in this stage of its life cycle for years.

The only way the cycle can proceed is if somewhere, relatively close by, there is another mycelium from another fungal spore of the same species growing in the same basic conditions. But here's the kicker: the neighboring fungal mycelium must be of the proper *mating type*. This is where my job gets a little complicated.

As a human being you are very familiar with the concept of sex. You are either a male or a female, and you understand that in order to reproduce, you must join forces with a member of the opposite sex. Well, mushrooms are stuck in the same predicament, except for the fact that they don't really have opposite sexes per se. Humans have male and female sexes. Mushrooms have positive (+) and negative (-) mating types.

There is absolutely no visible difference between (+) and (-) hyphae, but each requires the presence of its opposite if reproduction is to be possible. So if ten fungal spores of the (+) mating type all land on the same log in a forest, and each grows into a primary mycelium, none of them will be able to proceed to the next stage of the cycle.

If, however, just one of those spores is a (-) mating type, and the primary mycelium of a (+) mating type randomly bumps into it as it grows, things can start to happen. Somewhere in a rotten log, a (+) hypha will find a (-) hypha and they will join. Suddenly, the new cell that results has two nuclei, and as it divides into new cells, they too will each have two nuclei.

Each of the original primary mycelia will remain as they were, but the new hyphae with two nuclei in each cell will quickly grow into a new *secondary mycelium*. Wherever the fungal spores were growing (in dead wood, dead leaves, or even dead animals), the secondary mycelium will quickly head for the surface. Drawing on the primary mycelia in the same manner that a plant draws on its roots for resources, the secondary mycelium will emerge and become the only part of the fungus that we can actually see. Some mushrooms can simply appear overnight. This is because the conditions that allow the mushroom to form have been a long time in coming and the fungi need to get on with it. Each mushroom starts out looking something like an egg. Then the 'eggshell' tears and the little mushroom extends upward and unfolds like an umbrella.

Every cell in the mushroom still has two separate nuclei, but there are some very special cells that line the 'gills' on the underside of the mushroom's cap that are getting ready for reproduction. Inside little saclike structures the two haploid nuclei finally join into a single diploid nucleus. This is the same basic process as the union of egg and sperm cells, but in the case of a mushroom it can do this millions of times all at once.

The 'fertilized' diploid cells remain diploid only long enough for some genetic shuffling to occur, and then they divide again into haploid cells that are packaged into little shells. Yes, once again we have spores. At this point the spores are released out into the world in waves of millions upon millions in the hope that a few will land in a suitable place.

The thing to remember is that any mushroom you see represents only about 10 percent of the actual mass of the fungi involved. A single mushroom could be compared to an apple on an apple tree. The only real feat of imagination would be to picture the tree growing underground and sticking only its apples above ground.

The work of finding food requires that the hyphae of the fungi penetrate and infiltrate the particular food source that a given species requires, and competition has produced some very finicky mushrooms. Some live only on old hemlock logs, while others find only dead birch trees acceptable.

Then of course there is the complicated fact that the fungi kingdom can be divided into five separate phyla, only two of which produce anything even remotely close to a mushroom during their life cycles. All mushrooms are fungi, but not all fungi produce mushrooms.

Yellow chanterelle.

The single most iconic image of a mushroom is probably one with a white stalk and a red cap. It's easy to draw, easy to color, and as it happens it's also relatively easy to find. In fact there are several red mushrooms out there, but the one that I think best represents this archetype is a species called the emetic russula. Actually, there is a group of very similar species that fall into the genus *Russula,* and it can be very difficult to tell them apart unless you have a microscope. Nonetheless, these cute little mushrooms tend to emerge in August and September and are quite lovely to see. Beware, however, for most *Russula* species are poisonous and should never be eaten.

Another gorgeous species is the chanterelle *(Chantherellus cibarius).* This beautiful mushroom emerges from June to September and can be found singly or in groups growing under oaks or conifers. This species is also highly prized among mushroom hunters because it is delicious. Once again I must warn you to be . very cautious, however, because there are toxic look-alikes out there, and mushroom poisoning is a rather horrible way to go.

Now, most mushrooms seem to be white, brown, yellow, or red, but there are a few notable, and extremely beautiful, exceptions. One of these is a stunning species known as the indigo milky *(Lactarius indigo).* To my knowledge my grandmother never saw one of these, and I have seen only one example in my entire life. It was located on the south slope of the Holyoke Range State Park (in western Massachusetts), and it was growing in the middle of a mountain bike path that I was exploring.

To my knowledge this is the only bright blue mushroom out there, and try as I might I have never been able to find another one. This undoubtedly has a lot to do with the reproductive strategy of mushrooms, which produces mushrooms in a rather random pattern across the landscape in any given year.

You would also think that purple would be a fairly rare mushroom color, but believe it or not, it is actually more common than blue. There is one species that I have run across that really showcases the color purple, and that is the violet cort *(Cortinarius violaceus).* This one doesn't emerge until September or October, but you can find it easily enough if you look near decomposing logs in coniferous forests.

Finally, to finish off our look at different kinds of mushrooms, I thought I would showcase what I consider to be the most spectacular mushroom of all: the American Caesar's mushroom *(Amanita caesarea)*. A relative of one of my grandmother's favorite mushrooms (the deadly amanita), this species features an explosion of red, orange, and yellow with a beautiful veil on its stalk.

The American Caesar's mushroom emerges from July to October and can be found growing singly or in "fairy rings." Unlike many other species, it tends to grow in drier soils and is closely associated with oaks and pines. I happened to see a particularly beautiful example of the species growing on the side of a road in the town of Florida, Massachusetts, some years ago, and I simply had to stop and photograph it.

I could go on and on about the different types of mushrooms and how they differ, but that might be too much of a good thing. For now I will simply suggest that you go out and find yourself a mushroom (either in the woods or on a pizza) and give it some contemplation. The world is a rich, beautiful, and sometimes even delicious place if only you take the time to enjoy it.

Moose

I have crossed paths with moose many times in the past, but almost every one of those encounters took place before I started my career as a wildlife photographer. In 1991 I spent a summer up in the White Mountain National Forest, where I saw sign of moose almost every day. In 1999–2000, when I worked at Savoy Mountain State Forest (in western Massachusetts), I regularly saw moose sign, and in 2006 I took my wife back into the White

A male moose is just starting to grow his antlers.

Mountains with the goal of showing her a moose. I was able to find one for her, but the conditions at the time prevented me from getting a photo.

In the summer of 2007, however, I dedicated myself to finding my elusive quarry and, with photos in mind, I headed up to the heart of moose country—Maine. My brother had assured me that he could take me to a place where moose were seen as commonly as the white-tailed deer in my neighborhood. It took about an hour of slow driving and constant vigilance, but we eventually found our moose, and almost immediately I noticed something a little odd about him.

This male suffered an injury to the delicate tissues that
will become antlers. Note that he is missing a large portion
of the antler on the right side of this photo.

I could tell he was a 'him' because he had the beginnings of antlers growing in front of his ears. What was odd, however, was the fact that one of his antlers seemed to have been damaged. This probably impacted his ability to mate that season, but as you will see, he probably had many chances in the years that followed.

Antlers are the most conspicuous sexual characteristic of the deer family. Grown only by males, antlers have but one purpose, and that is fighting. The moose is the largest member of the deer family, and a large male (known as a "bull") can stand up to 7½ feet tall at the shoulder and can weigh up to 1,600 pounds. As you can imagine, bull moose are very well armed with huge antlers.

Antlers start growing in April and do not reach full size until August. During this time they are very fragile and resemble a honeycomb full of complex systems of blood vessels that deliver minerals to the growing tissues. Any damage to the antlers at the early stages of growth can prevent them from developing properly.

While growing, the antlers are covered with a thin layer of skin called "velvet," and in September, when the antlers have reached their full size, the bulls scrape them against bushes and trees to remove the velvet and polish the bone underneath. Traces of the veins and arteries can be seen on the surface of the antlers, which may have a span of 6 feet and can weigh up to 90 pounds!

From September to late October bulls become distracted with the rutting season, and they start fighting. They stop eating entirely, become very irritable, and spend all of their time trying to find females (known as "cows"). Unlike the males of many other species of deer, a bull moose does not collect and defend a harem during the rut. Instead he will find a single cow, defend her for about a week, and then go in search of another.

In January, when the breeding season is over and the antlers lose their value, the bulls finally shed their antlers, which serve as a popular source of minerals for chipmunks, mice, and other rodents. Bulls remain antlerless for the next few months before they finally start growing another pair the following April. In the meantime, the females carry their babies (called "calves") for eight months and usually give birth to twins in May or June. Unlike the young of other deer species, moose calves do not have white spots. The youngsters can walk only minutes after being born, and the cows become extremely protective of them. They will attack any threat, whether real or imagined, with powerful kicks from their front hooves. The calves grow quickly and are weaned at about six months of age. They spend the winter with their mothers and are then driven off just before the calving season of the following year.

Moose are still relatively uncommon in the southern portions of the Northeast, but they are staging a comeback that mirrors the return of the raven, the turkey, the black bear, and the coyote. This, in a nutshell, is what has happened:

During the Pleistocene period (over a million years ago) the ancestors of the modern moose crossed into North America from Siberia. This was made possible because huge amounts of water were locked into spreading ice sheets during one of the great glaciation events of that time and the level of the oceans slowly dropped.

Eventually the Bering Sea (between Siberia and Alaska) dropped enough to expose a land bridge, which many ancient mammals (including the moose) used as a gateway to the New World. By the time the first humans arrived in North America (the jury is still out on the exact date, but it was probably 40 thousand to 50 thousand years ago), the moose was common across Canada and the northern United States.

Prior to European colonization, moose were common in the eastern US as far south as Virginia, but by the mid-1800s the colonists had dramatically changed the landscape. In Massachusetts, for example, 70 percent of the land had been converted into agricultural fields. As a result of this large-scale habitat loss and heavy hunting pressures, moose were extirpated (driven into local extinction). Today the conditions are reversed and about 70 percent of Massachusetts is forested once again. Many of the animals that had been extirpated have made comebacks, and moose are finally among them.

Moose sightings have been increasing steadily, and this was illustrated just a few weeks prior to my trip to Maine. Before leaving on my adventure, I met up with my friends John and Merry Cushing for a trip to a local wildlife reserve. We had a wonderful time exploring the ponds and forest trails in the reserve, but that afternoon (after I was home) I got a call from my mother—there was a moose in town and I had missed it.

I had been in the right place, with the right equipment, and with the right people, but not at the right time. That weekend I heard stories of moose, turkeys, and bear being seen right in my hometown. I, on the other hand, managed to get a picture of a frog. Not quite the same, is it?

With any luck the return of the moose will continue as the years flood past us. Perhaps the sighting of a moose foraging in a roadside marsh will become as common as spying a flock of wild turkeys or catching sight of a raven gliding across distant treetops. It is a nice thought to contemplate, and I shall remain ever vigilant for signs of these large, secretive denizens of the forest.

The Gray Catbird

Being a scientist, with all of the compulsions that entails, I cannot refrain from keeping lists. I keep a daily journal of events that transpire outside, I keep lists of blooming times for flowers and weather events, and (of course) I keep a list of the different bird species I can either see or hear in my yard. I have no idea if this information will ever be valuable, but I just can't seem to stop myself.

More than anything, the information I record is fun to look back at because it helps me remember simple things that happened. For instance, my journal entry from June 11, 2006, reads, "Went out to take photos of lightning as it was getting dark. Took five rolls; best photo was frame 25 on last roll. The rabbits were playing their courtship leapfrog game, bullfrogs and tree frogs were singing, song sparrows and catbirds were making quite a ruckus, and the little hummingbird was coming very close to me as I was sitting on the porch."

This excerpt captures just a little slice of the coming summer that year, but one of the elements that I find impossible to ignore is the gray catbird. This wonderful species is a ubiquitous inhabitant of the summer landscape, but I feel that it rarely gets the full credit it is due for the amount of joy that it can bring to anyone's day.

Before I get started with the up-close-and-personal examination of the gray catbird, why don't I dispense with the purely scientific information? Actually, it just so happens that the gray catbird's scientific name, *Dumtella carolinensis*, is a great one for leading into a discussion of the natural history of this engaging little bird.

The word *Dumtella* is of Latin origin. The word *dumus* means "a thorn bush," and the suffix *ella* is diminutive in nature. Thus, the word *Dumtella* can be translated as "the little one of the thorn bush." This is a great description for a catbird because catbirds love thickets. The word *carolinensis* is simply a Latinized form of the word *Carolina*, which was probably added because the catbird was first discovered in the Carolinas. If that hasn't got you cheering for catbirds, I don't really know what's wrong with you.

Catbirds spend half their time in the north, half their time in the south, and half their time traveling between the two. Wait . . . they spend half their time in the north, two-thirds of their time traveling, and one-third of their time in the south. No . . . they spend eight-sixteenths of their time in the south, 150 days in the north, and eight weeks traveling. Actually . . . they spend fourteen . . . oh forget it!

Catbirds arrive in our area at the beginning of May. Males will look for a nice piece of prime catbird real estate, which can include dense brush, shrubland, wooded suburban areas, and even the edges of forests. Ideally, catbirds would find a patchwork landscape of lawns, fields, and thickets to be perfect, which is why catbirds are so abundant around human homes. Catbirds never venture into deep forests.

Once a male has a claim on a territory, he goes about the process of attracting a mate. In the world of the catbird, this involves quite an elaborate ritual. The male will chase the female (yeah, like she's really trying to get away) and then will pause to sing for her. This would be an outstanding opportunity for the female to get away, but she always stops to listen. (I told you . . . nudge nudge, wink wink.)

And why not? Catbirds are members of the mimic thrush family and are outstanding songsters. They can be identified by their energetic, squeaky impersonations of other birds, but their catlike calls are the surefire sign of their presence. Both male and female do the cat calls, but only the male sings.

Whilst he sings, he will strut his stuff in a very provocative manner. He will lower his wings so they almost drag on the ground, he will hold his tail up in the air, and occasionally (and this is really bold of him) he will turn around so the female can get a gander at his rusty-red undertail covert feathers. Ladies, this has the same effect on female catbirds as a tuxedoed George Clooney or a bare-chested Hugh Jackman might have on you. Needless to say, once a male catbird gets his mojo working, there is little that can stop him.

After sweeping the female off her feet, the male catbird actually proves himself to be a very faithful, hard-working part-

A gray catbird.

ner. The male assists with nest building, but it is the female that selects the spot and sees to most of the details. Male catbirds, like so many other male birds, are usually very busy defending a territory, and they need to be flexible so they can respond to any incursions.

The nest is generally located from three to ten feet off the ground in thick vegetation. The nest is cup-shaped and can include such materials as grass, twigs, leaves, and finer material to line the inside of the cup. In my experience, if there are grapevines anywhere in the vicinity, then catbirds always incorporate strips of grapevine bark in their nests.

Once the nest is complete, the female sets about the task of laying a clutch of two to six beautiful blue eggs. She lays one a day and does not commence incubation until the last egg is laid, which ensures that all of the eggs will hatch at the same time. The eggs are very vulnerable during the laying period, but once incubation starts, the female will sit tight and do her best to hide them from predators. The male does his best to make sure predators don't even get close.

The eggs hatch after twelve to thirteen days, and the babies then need an additional ten to eleven days before they can fledge. Because they live in such dense vegetation, baby catbirds can leave the nest well before they are able to fly with any great skill. Fluttering through a thicket is more than adequate, but sitting still and being very quiet is always the best course of action for young birds.

Once they have fledged, the male takes an active role in feeding the babies. The female may even start a second nest while he cares for their youngsters, and by the time they are done, there could be up to ten young catbirds running around a successful territory. After that, time is all that is needed.

Catbirds winter as far south as Panama, and young catbirds need time to grow and perfect their flying. By the end of October all of the catbirds will be gone, and we will have to wait another season before we once again hear those squeaky songs and catlike calls coming from the bushes.

Moths by the Porch Light

At this moment a small radio-controlled car is sending a tiny radio signal across the void of space in an attempt to tell us what the conditions on the fourth rock from the sun (also known as Mars) are like. We know that Mars is roughly half the size of Earth; we have learned that the average temperature on Mars is 64 degrees below zero and that the red planet is a lot more like Earth than we ever suspected. But the big question remains, "Will life be found?" NASA has spent billions in an effort to answer this question. A simple speck of life would 'change' our lives forever. Isn't it interesting, then, that all of this is happening while we here on Earth are surrounded by more life than we know what to do with? Why is the possibility of life on Mars more interesting than the hundreds of millions of living things just outside our doors?

This evening I want you to go out onto your porch, look up into the sky, and try to locate Mars. Do you think you can find it? I'm not sure I could. It might not be out, it might be the wrong time of day, or the wrong time of year to see the red planet. Even if it is out, it is just a point of light in a sky filled with countless other points of light. It is out of reach, not of our world. But instead of going in and watching CNN or the NASA channel, I want you to walk over to the porch light and take a look at the animals that will gather there. Odds are that you will be the only mammal that has been attracted to the light, and you will be in the company of a multitude of insects. Insects belong to the larger group of arthropods, which also includes animals such as lobsters, crabs, scorpions, spiders, and centipedes. Of all animal life on Earth, arthropods are by far the most numerous and diverse. They live in almost every habitat on land and under the surface of Earth's waters, but it is the insects that are perhaps the most familiar to all of us.

The insects have been the most successful group of animals to ever inhabit the Earth, and they surely owe a great measure of their success to the simple fact that they can fly. They were the first living things that could fly, and when they first started flying, more than 240 million years ago, they were able to gain access to habitats that were almost completely uninhabited by any other forms of animal life. They were the first to colonize

A rosy maple moth.

the land and have remained dominant in numbers ever since. It has been estimated that there are 1,000,000,000,000,000,000 insects alive at any one time. In the peak of summer, when insect numbers are at their highest here in the Northeast, there may be as many as 50 million insects sitting, crawling, hopping, and flying over every square mile of land. They are everywhere, and they are glorious.

The insects that you will most readily recognize while you stand next to the porch light will probably be the moths. Moths are very closely related to butterflies, and together the two

Anther species shows cryptic camouflage in the shape and color of its wings.

groups form the order *Lepidoptera*. There are at least 125 thousand known species of moths and butterflies in the world, and in North America we have 12 thousand known species. These insects have long been admired for their often spectacular wings, and butterflies in particular have developed some extraordinary colors. Moths tend to be drabber since they are active mostly at night (bright colors do no good in the dark). As flashy as many butterflies are, however, it may interest you to know that of the 12 thousand known species of Lepidoptera in North America, only about 760 of them are butterflies. That leaves over 11 thousand species of moths!

Moths come in all sizes, from the very large luna moths to extremely tiny and obscure species that don't even have common names. But if you take a look at the moths by your light, you will be in for a treat! Most moths have to hide during the day, and their wings have evolved to help them do this. Unlike butterflies, which hold their wings up while they rest, moths hold their wings flat to their sides in an effort to smooth out their profile and hide their bodies from view. In many cases, a particular species of moth has evolved to mimic a specific kind of tree bark or other background, and when motionless the moths will be invisible.

When you consider how many different species of plants there are, it is easy to see how there can be so many different moths. Each species of moth lives a slightly different life, eating slightly different parts of slightly different plants. They each have their own 'niche,' and each species tries to blend in with some part of its surroundings. Some look like dead leaves, others like living leaves. Some look like a spot of lichen on tree bark, and there is even one group of moths that are active in the day and look and behave just like hummingbirds. Just take a look at any moth and try to decide what it is trying to look like. Odds are that if you go out the next day, and look in a place that features that kind of object, you will find the very kind of moth you saw, now sitting motionless and waiting for dark. This could make a great project for any family.

Turn off the TV, grab a pencil and paper for taking notes, turn on the porch light, and watch. Try to keep track of how many different kinds of moths you see, and you will quickly find yourself tallying over fifty species. There are several good moth identification guides that can help you, and your library may have one you can borrow for an evening. Just remember two things: First, moths are attracted to lights more strongly on hot, muggy nights. On a clear, cool night you may see very few moths. Second, there are a lot of very tiny moths that will come to your light, and it is possible that one of them may belong to a species still unknown to science. With so many species and so few scientists with the expertise to identify them, some species have undoubtedly gone unnoticed. A friend of mine once started a small research project in which he looked through all of the insects that got caught in his light fixtures and picked out all of the tiny moths. In just one day he had amassed an impressive collection, and both of us knew that one of his moths might have been a new, unknown species.

While you are out looking at moths, keep a lookout for my personal favorite, the rosy maple moth. This is a small moth, maybe an inch long, but you could never miss it because it is bright yellow and pink. Whether you see one or not, you should have a great time looking at moths, and you can easily stimulate the minds and imaginations of your children in the process.

Bobolinks

I love thunderstorms. They rumble across the landscape in late May and early June like heralds announcing the approach of summer. Some years we have a few such storms, but others we have many. Sometimes we may even have a solid week filled with daily visits of these powerful reminders of Nature's dominion over the Earth. In such years my lawn will be oozing with water, and I will be convinced that if I can't get out with the mower, I'll have to use a machete to get through some of the taller stuff.

A bobolink.

I imagine that many of you may have the same concerns about your yards in such years, but just remember that there is a silver lining in these very dark rain clouds. The very same rain that prevents us from mowing our lawns is also postponing the haying schedule. While this is an annoyance for the farmers, it is the difference between life and death for some of our local birds.

The species I am speaking of most directly is the bobolink (*Dolichonyx oryzivorus*). The bobolink is a rather remarkable bird in the sense that its coloration is quite different from the norm. Most birds have a darker color above with a lighter color below, but the bobolink (at least the male) shows the opposite color scheme. Jet black below with white above is so interesting that it even provoked a comment from William Cullen Bryant in his poem "Robert of Lincoln":

> . . . Robert of Lincoln is gayly drest,
> Wearing a bright black wedding-coat;
> White are his shoulders and white his crest.
> Hear him call in his merry note:
> Bob-o'-link, bob-o'-link, Spink, spank, spink;
> Look, what a nice new coat is mine,
> Sure there was never a bird so fine.
> Chee, chee, chee.
>
> Robert of Lincoln's Quaker wife,
> Pretty and quiet, with plain brown wings,
> Passing at home a patient life,
> Broods in the grass while her husband sings:
> Bob-o'-link, bob-o'-link, Spink, spank, spink;
> Brood, kind creature; you need not fear
> Thieves and robbers while I am here.
> Chee, chee, chee . . .

No, I do not have a clear understanding of who Robert of Lincoln is. Suffice it to say that "Robert of Lincoln" becomes

"Bob of Lincoln," which can be further shortened to "Bob o' Linc," and ultimately "bobolink."

I do, however, understand the scientific name. *Dolichonyx* is a combination of the Greek word *dolichos*, which means "long," and the Greek *onux*, which means "claw." The species name *oryzivorus* is built upon the Latin word *oryzi*, meaning "rice." A meat-eating animal is said to be carnivorous, while the bobolink is clearly a rice-eater. Taken together, the entire name comes out to be "the long-clawed rice-eater." These are birds of open fields that have expanded their range eastward as a result of human activity.

A male bobolink in full song.

As flashy and interesting as this species is, few people seem to know much about it. I often suspect that people know less than they should about our wild neighbors, and I can recall an experience I had that seemed to support this suspicion at the time. As I recall, I was out running errands with my wife when I was overcome with a spontaneous desire to drive past my house and continue down the road to an area where two great hayfields are separated by a single, narrow road. I saw bobolinks everywhere, so I dashed home, freed my wife, and headed back with my cameras.

I pulled my car to the side of the road, rolled down the window, and set my largest lens on the door frame. It was just seconds before a beautiful, sassy bobolink flew over to my location and attempted to start a debate with me over who belonged in the field and who didn't. It was made quite clear that I was intruding and was not particularly welcome. My feelings were hurt, but I stubbornly stayed put.

A few moments later I began to understand the excited state of the male bobolink because I noticed a female fly in and land within 50 feet of my position. My camera was ready, I swung it in her direction, and when I focused on her, I saw that her beak was full of food. She had babies close by.

I even managed to get a glimpse of a movement out in the tall grass as she hopped down to feed her little ones. I never got an actual look at the babies, but I know they were there because both parents kept returning with food. I imagine that this field was literally packed with baby bobolinks, but they were completely hidden to anyone but their mothers.

The male spent most of his time in a flustery attempt to draw his youngsters away from me. He landed on the tallest bits of grass, waved his wings like a maniac, and kept up a constant barrage of call notes intended to have the same effect on his babies as the Pied Piper's song had on human children.

This excitable attitude was not reserved for me in any way, however. Any time a red-winged blackbird strayed into the male bobolink's airspace, he was driven off with great vigor. The male bobolink did not seem to mind the presence of the many tree swallows that crisscrossed the field, but I imagine that is because the swallows could not offer any sort of competition to the bobolink.

As I was quite close to the corner of one of the fields, I decided to pan the top of the grasses to see what other activity might be taking place closer to its center. I was quite surprised to see many other male bobolinks sitting at fairly regular intervals across the surface of the field. I say "surface" because I was struck by how much the field reminded me of a pond at that moment. The adult bobolinks spent most of their time on the surface of the grass, like ducks, and only occasionally dove down into the grass to capture food or feed babies.

Anyway, as I sat there with my camera, a woman in a passing car stopped to ask me what I was looking for. The big lens is a great icebreaker, and people always want to know what is going on. I told her I was looking at bobolinks, and even pointed the birds out to her, and she visibly had one of those moments where the world had just become a little more interesting. She even expressed a caring for wild animals when she said, "Gee, I hope the farmer doesn't mow the field." People who care are great!

Her concern was well founded. Every June, the fields across our area are full of baby birds. Most are near flying, but not quite there yet. If a field in such a state is mowed, and then the fresh cuttings dispersed with a spreader, all of the young birds will be killed. On many occasions I have seen despondent bobolinks circling over freshly mowed fields looking for babies that can no longer answer. At such times it is a simple fact that just one more week of rain might have given the babies a chance to fly before the mowers arrived. I keep my fingers crossed for rain every summer!

If we are lucky, and the baby bobolinks survive, they will spend the summer growing strong enough to participate in their species' amazing flights to South America, moving as far south as the Argentine Pampas! Then, with an even greater helping of luck, they will return next spring to fill our fields with their marvelous, bubbling songs.

The Bullfrog

It was a morning that started off surprisingly chilly for June. Temperatures down in the 50s led to a somewhat subdued dawn chorus, and as a result I stayed in bed longer than I had planned. My brother and I had thought the words "We'll meet at dawn" had a nice ring to them the previous evening, but they certainly lost their appeal when dawn finally arrived. The birds were quiet, the house was quiet, and both of us decided to sleep in.

At about 6:30 I finally felt enough shame to get out of bed. The birds outside had rubbed the sand out of their eyes and had at least attempted a morning performance. I got dressed quickly, slipped downstairs, and met my bleary-eyed, yet cheerful younger brother in the family room of my parents' house. It was Tom's birthday, and my entire family had converged in Amherst, Massachusetts, to celebrate. Everyone else in the family, however, appeared to have had the good sense to sleep in.

But the birds beckoned us onward, and in no time at all we were headed out the driveway. We headed west and entered a housing development that had been stopped in its tracks by the economy. Only the road had been built, and instead of houses, people, and their pets, the disturbed area made a lovely home for catbirds, song sparrows, and even a black-and-white warbler.

We spent about forty-five minutes chasing the birds around until we finally headed north on Middle Street and turned into the Plum Brook Conservation Area. This is a trip that Tom and I made many times when we were boys, but in those days we were just headed to Mallek's pond. What had once been a farm road is now a driveway. What had once been a series of small pastures is now a series of housing lots. The horses are gone, and the barn is gone, but Mallek's pond is still there, though it too is virtually unrecognizable.

The manmade pond has gone wild in the past twenty years or so. All traces of the artificial beach are gone, and the shoreline has increased in size and muddiness. Beavers have also created a beautiful wetland on the other side of the small road that still marks the position of the dam that formed the pond in the first place. The beaver pond is actually much larger than the one Mr. Mallek made, but Mr. Mallek's road is the only reason anyone can enjoy the wetlands and keep their feet dry at the same time.

Tom and I slowly walked out between the two ponds, wordlessly agreed on a good place to stop, and just soaked in the surroundings. It was still early enough so the sun was low in the sky, and there was just the slightest mist rising off the water. Young cattails were about halfway through their growth, and they emerged from the water in the company of bullhead lilies and water striders.

A male oriole teased us with his brief appearance in a small tree. Just enough time to show us he was there, but not enough to swing cameras in his direction. Then, in the beaver pond, we spotted a pair of pileated woodpeckers foraging together in a dead tree. As with many beaver ponds, there had one time been an abundance of dead trees. Wind, ice, and time have caused most of them to topple over, but a few still stand straight out of the water like the bleached rib bones of some great whale that died in antiquity.

The scene was perfect. With smiles on both our faces, my brother and I commented on how it just couldn't get much better than this, and it was just at that moment that a final ingredient was added to the mix. From the cattails growing on what used to be Mr. Mallek's beach came the sonorous song of a bullfrog.

Suddenly, it was summer! The chill in the air seemed to slip away, and memories of hunting for tadpoles filled both our heads. There was no chance to jump into the water on this particular morning, but we decided to hunt for the frog the way any respectable adult would . . . with binoculars. While we looked, we heard another bullfrog start singing, and then another. Bull-frogs, however, are not particularly easy to find.

The largest of our frogs, the bullfrog (*Rana catesbiana*) is also the most aquatic. Unlike green frogs and pickerel frogs, which both explore dry land in search of food, bullfrogs rarely leave the water for any reason. Only during prolonged periods of rain will bullfrogs go on walkabout, searching for new ponds to colonize. The rest of the time bullfrogs are homebodies.

Although they can change the color of their skins, bullfrogs are most often seen in their green uniforms of mid-summer. In fact, they are almost the same color as bullhead lilies, with their backs the same color as the lily pads, and the throats of the

A male bullfrog skulks in the cattails.

males the same color as the lily flowers themselves. This coloration makes it very difficult to find bullfrogs, but Tom and I finally spotted two or three.

I turned my big lens toward the closest of the frogs and decided that I would just wait for a while. He was particularly active, and I was determined to get photos of the frog with a huge, distended throat while he sang his song. In her wonderful publication "The Frog Book," Mary C. Dickerson describes the bullfrog's song as, "Jug 'o rum, jug 'o rum, more rum." Whatever the frog really says, it is also proclaiming that summer has arrived.

It took about ten minutes, but I finally managed to get a photo of the frog in the middle of his song. His bright yellow throat didn't balloon out as much as that of a toad would have, but it was still much larger than that of an idle bullfrog. Although I never managed to see any of the other frogs in the middle of their songs, I was able to count about seven different individuals in the chorus at its peak.

As the summer matures and temperatures steadily rise, the songs of bullfrogs will become more prominent. Long after the spring peepers and American toads have fallen silent, bullfrogs will continue to sing. Particularly during the nighttime hours, the songs of bullfrogs can travel great distances and add a particularly beautiful quality to the landscape.

Imagine a warm, balmy evening with a few clouds in the sky. The moon is out, the stars are twinkling in the heavens, and the crickets are just beginning to add their voices to the nighttime chorus. A warm breeze pushes a cloud in front of the moon, and the landscape is dark for a moment. Then, from off in the distance, a single bullfrog calls out into the night in a low, booming voice that carries in the humid air.

As the moon reappears from behind the cloud, another bullfrog starts to sing. In the absence of cars, TVs, and the confusion of the human world, we describe this scene with all of its amphibian noise as being "quiet." I encourage everyone to turn off the TV, step out into the moonlight, and enjoy the quiet this summer. Shut off the air conditioner, open up the windows, and let the bullfrog songs that float in the nighttime air be your summertime lullaby.

The Ruby-throated Hummingbird

One of the most entertaining aspects of summer is getting to know the new birds, mammals, insects, reptiles, and amphibians that live in the area that I call "my yard." To them, it is probably their yard, and I suppose it would be fair to say that I am simply one of the animals whose territory overlaps theirs. It's a little humbling to think of life on these terms, but rather exciting too. I feel connected to the Earth.

Down in the woods roams a family of coyotes. I hear them almost every night, but haven't seen any of them yet. In the same forest a doe and her fawns also live. I have seen them on several occasions, and the fawns are growing up quickly. Soon it will be difficult to tell them apart from their mother, and she will surely wish that she had taken more pictures when they were just babies.

A family of raccoons has been causing a predictable level of mischief on my porch at night. I have to bring in my bird-feeders as soon as it gets dark or they are subjected to vigorous examinations and abuse. I also have a small aquarium on my porch where I am keeping some snails and water plants for the summer. Every night the raccoons probe the depths of this small tank, looking for who knows what, and leaving muddy foot-prints all along the length of my deck.

There are frogs that live in the tall grass that I have left by a wet spot in the back yard. There are also snakes that patrol this area, presumably looking for the frogs. And everywhere in the lawn there are the neat, tubular tunnels made by voles. Like little subway systems, these tunnels are maintained by the voles and undoubtedly connect all of the most important places in the voles' lives. It is always fun to sit and watch a patch of grass until a furry little subway car makes its frantic way to wherever it deems important to get to at the time.

One of the highlights of any summer evening is the song of katydids in the trees and grasses around my house, but here are innumerable other insects flying, hopping, and crawling around. There are field crickets in the garage, moths by the porch light at night, and butterflies that come to sip nectar from the wildflowers in my lawn. Bumblebees and honeybees collect nectar from the clover, spider killers (a group of wasps) stalk the sides of the house looking for victims, and yellow jackets swarm around the hummingbird feeder.

Then, of course, there are the hummingbirds for whom I put the feeder out. More than any other creatures, I think the hummingbirds have provided the most delightful moments. Their antics are fast, frantic, and flashy, but because they are so confident in their ability to escape any sort of danger, they are also relatively fearless of humans and are quite willing to go about their daily lives right out in the open.

There is one adult male hummingbird who tried, at least for a time, to claim the feeder for himself. He is loud, fidgety,

A male ruby-throated hummingbird feeds from a beebalm flower.

and quite put out by the idea of sharing. Then there is an adult female that comes to the feeder regularly. She is all business. There is no displaying or fighting with her. She just zips in from the northeast, tanks up on sugar water, and takes off again.

The antics that have proven most delightful, however, are those of the babies. Young hummingbirds are inquisitive and quite fearless, which makes them wonderful to watch. Hum-

This male ruby-throated hummingbird declared
himself king of the feeders.

mingbirds in general seem so confident of their flying skills that they are willing to come quite close to people anyway. So, when you add in the factors of inexperience and being a little on the goofy side, young hummingbirds are a scream. The most entertaining moments have been those provided by the young males. They are all practicing the territoriality that they will need as adults, and because they are so evenly matched, they spend what seem to be hours hovering, displaying, and chasing one another around. I think the abundance of food in the form of sugar water from the feeders has allowed them to spend more time playing than they would normally be able to.

But one of the young males seems to be making his mark, and he even dares to sit atop the potted fig tree that I have on my porch. This perch gives him a perfect view of the feeder and the comings and goings of any interlopers through his airspace. He is king of the roost until the adult male returns and soundly dethrones him with stunning swiftness. The old male is clearly in charge and exercises his will wherever and whenever he pleases.

For those of you who don't already know, the hummingbirds in our area are all of a single species—the ruby-throated hummingbird (*Achilochus colubris*). Worldwide there are somewhere between 319 and 339 true species, and many hybrids.

All hummingbirds are found in the New World, and the majority of these species are found in the tropical regions of South America. There are only twenty-one species that can be found in the U.S., only eight that range up any distance from the Mexican border, and only three that can be found in Canada. Here in the Northeast there is only one species, the ruby-throated.

The name of our hummingbird comes as no surprise when you actually see a male. Hummingbirds have feathers that can refract light, giving them a decidedly metallic look. Their backs are the color of glimmering emeralds, and their throats, when seen in the proper light, flare up like burning rubies. Females lack the ruby throats, but keep the emerald sheen across their dorsal surfaces.

Ruby-throated hummingbirds are strongly attracted to the color red, which explains why so many hummingbird feeders have red plastic components, and why commercial hummingbird foods have red dye added to them. I will tell you now, however, that the commercial foods are expensive and not at all good for the hummingbirds because they often include preservatives that are harmful to adults and babies alike.

To make your own hummingbird food, mix one cup of boiling water with ¼ cup of white sugar. Let it cool to room temperature and then put it in your feeder. Remember to change the water every couple of days so that mold will not build up in the nectar. The red plastic parts of the feeder will be more than sufficient to capture the birds' interest. If you want to have some fun, try sitting next to a hummingbird feeder while you are wearing something red. Most likely you will see the bird come to your feeder, take a sip of sugar water, and then zip down to take a closer look at you.

Hummingbirds are a real treat, but they do not linger late in the summer. Mid-September is as late in the year as most of us in the Northeast can hope to see hummingbirds, and then they head off to Mexico for the winter. This is an amazing journey for a bird that measures only 3½ inches long and weighs about 4 grams (there are 28 grams in an ounce!).

So if you have the chance to spend any time with humming-birds in your neck of the woods, do it! Spend as much time as you can watching their wonderful little lives because they disappear as suddenly as they appear in the spring. When they do finally leave, other amazing birds will arrive, however, so don't abandon your watching spot.

FALL

An eastern chipmunk sits atop my woodpile.

Woodpile Wildlife

Every year my firewood arrives in the same manner: two cords
of seasoned oak, maple, and ash in a large, jumbled pile on the
lawn. I think that everyone will agree that burning the wood is
nice. You can enjoy the crackle of a fire in a fireplace, or soak up
the heat radiating out of a wood stove on a chilly morning. But
getting the wood stacked before the snow falls is far less pleasant. That does not mean that it can't be interesting, though.

There is actually a lot going on in woodpiles, and since all
of my wood-burning brothers and sisters out there will have
to spend time moving them, organizing them, and then taking
them apart, layer by layer, we might as well learn something in
the process. So as you sit with your coffee, preparing to go stack
wood, let me introduce you to some of the wildlife that you may
soon encounter.

First off, there are five groups of animal life that you are
likely to encounter as you work. In order of probable abundance, they are: 1) arthropods, 2) mollusks, 3) amphibians, 4)
mammals, and 5) reptiles. As you start to move your wood, you
will notice that there are very few signs of life. The upper layers
of the pile are too warm, dry, and exposed for most of the wildlife in your woodpile, but there is one little beast that you might
come across . . . the daddy-longlegs.

These animals belong to the phylum *Arthropoda*. Arthropods are a group of animals usually referred to as "bugs" and
include insects, spiders, and a very small number of species from
the crustacean family which inhabit terrestrial habitats. While
most people think of daddy-longlegs as spiders, which belong to

the order *Araneae*, they are in fact members of a separate order, *Opilones*, and often referred to as "harvestmen." Why harvestmen? The first specimens of this order were observed during the autumn. Autumn is harvest time, and thus the name *harvestman* was adopted.

There are 3,500 species of daddy-longlegs worldwide, with over 200 species in North America. The two most common species are the eastern and the brown. These arthropods are mainly nocturnal and hunt many other arthropods such as spiders, flies, aphids, and leafhoppers. Other prey items include earthworms, snails, and the gills of fungi. These animals are completely harmless to humans and should not be smashed on sight.

No matter how warm and dry the upper layers of the woodpile are, the bottom of the pile will always be cooler and more humid. These conditions, combined with lower light levels, create ideal conditions for the growth of fungi, which in turn provide food for other animals. As soon as you get to the bottom of the pile, you will notice a huge increase in life forms.

One of the most familiar of these is the slug, a terrestrial gastropod mollusk. *Mollusk* is the common name for soft-bodied animals that usually create a hard shell for their protection. The word *mollusk* is derived from the Latin word *mollus*, which means "soft." Other familiar members of this phylum are clams, oysters, snails, squid, and octopuses.

Gastropods are mollusks, which are generally characterized by a single shell and an asymmetric body. Numbering some 37,500 species, these animals form the second largest class in the animal kingdom, outnumbered only by insects. The word *gastropod* is derived from the Greek words *gaster*, meaning "stomach," and *pous*, meaning "foot." Aside from the shell, there isn't much more to a gastropod than a stomach and a big foot.

Young slugs usually have well-developed shells, but as the slug grows, it either sheds the shell or keeps it as a small remnant. Slugs are vegetarians and move around the lower levels of your woodpile in search of different kinds of fungi to eat. Their movement is assisted by mucous, which they produce in a gland at the front of their foot. Slugs cannot survive long in dry conditions, however, so you will rarely see them out in the open unless it has recently rained.

Another interesting critter you may come across is a sow bug. These animals are the small, gray, shield-shaped 'bugs' that like to live under the pieces of wood at the bottom of the pile. They can be found in large groups, and they resemble trilobites.

Sow bugs are actually *isopods*, a subset of the class *Crustacea* of the arthropod phylum. The majority of crustaceans are actually aquatic, and sow bugs are more closely related to lobsters and crayfish than anything else. They are one of a very few members of their class that have evolved to live on land.

Another interesting animal you might find is a millipede. These guys are relatively slow-moving animals that feed on plants or other decaying material. Depending on the species, millipedes may have from nine to more than one hundred body segments, with two pairs of simple legs on each segment. Their main defensive strategy is to curl up into a ball and secrete a foul-smelling fluid. Millipedes that are successful in protecting themselves may live up to seven years.

A sowbug sits next to a pair of salamander eggs.

Centipedes can also be found at the bottom of the wood-pile, but unlike millipedes, centipedes are fast-moving predators. Centipedes have fewer legs than millipedes, and their bodies are much flatter. This allows them to move into small spaces quickly while they chase after prey. Once they catch something, they grab it with their first pair of legs, which act like venomous jaws. Although they are generally harmless to humans, a few tropical species can inflict painful bites.

Insects are the largest and most familiar class of the phylum *Arthropoda*. With more than one million species, they are also the most numerous form of animal life on the planet. Insects have six legs and three body sections, and most have wings. They are perhaps the most successful life form in existence, with the first primitive representatives appearing about 350 million years ago. With so many species to choose from, it would be impossible for me to describe all of the potential woodpile insects in this article, but let me describe two of the most frequently seen insects for you.

The woolly bear is a common, and very well-known, inhabitant of woodpiles, and it is a member of what is probably the most popular of the insect orders, the butterflies. The woolly bear is actually the caterpillar (larva) of the Isabella tiger moth, an incredibly beautiful moth with bold white and black wing patterns and pink underwings. This species spends the winter in the caterpillar stage, and that is why we find it in our woodpiles so late in the year.

There is a cute little bit of folklore that suggests that you can predict the severity of the coming winter by measuring the length of the brown section of a woolly bear. In truth, however, the woolly bear starts out with more black than brown, and with each successive molt the brown band gets broader. So in fact, the brown band is only good for estimating the age of the caterpillar and tells us nothing of the winter to come.

Finally, there are those little black beetles that skitter around the ground after the wood has all been moved. These little guys will often run as far as the first piece of bark, and then try to hide until you rake the area and uncover them.

These beetles have been assigned the very unimaginative name of *common black ground beetle*. I guess the challenge of coming up with one million names requires that some be fairly boring. Most beetles are capable of living out in the open, and the common black ground beetle is no exception, but it hunts caterpillars, grubs, and other soft-bodied insects that live in the lowest layers of woodpiles. As with so many other animals, the common black ground beetle is drawn in by the availability of food.

For any of my readers, particularly younger people, who may not be terribly familiar with the terms *vertebrate* and *invertebrate*, let me offer this explanation: Life on Earth is divided into six kingdoms—the plants, animals, fungi, protists, eubacteria and archaebacteria. All of the millions of members of the animal kingdom are then assigned to progressively smaller groupings—phyla, classes, orders, families, genera, and finally species.

The process of evolution has produced many ground-breaking developments that have allowed different animals to take advantage of previously unexploited habitats. One of the most ancient of these developments in the animal kingdom was the growth of an internal skeleton to support the body. It started in the oceans with boneless fish, and it took hundreds of millions of years for this 'development' to take place, but eventually fish with skeletons were swimming in the Earth's oceans.

Some of the new bones were formed around the long bundle of nerves that ran down the length of the bodies of the fish. We call these bones "vertebrae," and the entire grouping is known as the "vertebral column." Are the terms *vertebrate* and *invertebrate* starting to make sense yet?

This development was so ancient that it has been recorded at the phylum level. Animals with bones are members of the *Chordata* phylum, and are known to us as vertebrates, whereas animals without bones are known as invertebrates. Examples of vertebrates are birds, mammals, reptiles, amphibians, and fish. So let's take a look at some of the vertebrate animals that might be living in or around your woodpile.

As with the invertebrates, most of the vertebrates are going to be found in the lower levels of the woodpile. There is, however, one rambunctious vertebrate you are likely to see as it perches atop the peak of your woodpile. Any guesses as to its identity? Okay, here are a few hints: it is a mammal, it is small, loud, fast, and a lot of fun to watch. Now can you guess? Correct! It is the eastern chipmunk.

Woodpiles are a valuable resource for any chipmunk fleeing from a predator. The loosely assembled pieces of wood provide many corridors for escape, or the chipmunk can simply hang out for a while until the predator gives up. It may surprise you to learn that chipmunks also eat many kinds of invertebrates (such as slugs) that live in woodpiles.

The other mammals that might live in your woodpile are white-footed mice, voles, shrews, and weasels. As with chipmunks, a woodpile can be a valuable feature in the territory of a white-footed mouse. A woodpile provides it with good hiding places and a fairly reliable source of invertebrate prey, but it may also be a dangerous place if there are any weasels living nearby.

A long-tailed weasel visits a woodpile in search of food.

Weasels are efficient hunters, and because of their size and shape, they can pursue mice, voles, and chipmunks even in the relative safety of a woodpile. It is unlikely that a female weasel would ever choose to build a nest in a woodpile, but she would certainly patrol the area to look for food.

There are a few amphibians that you might find as you move your wood. One of the most abundant of these is the red-backed salamander. It may be that you never would have thought of a salamander as a vertebrate, but they do in fact have little skeletons which are actually remarkably similar to our own.

The red-backed salamander is a member of the *Plethodontidae*, or lungless salamander family. The largest family of salamanders, with some 215 species, it is thought to have originated in the Northeastern United States. Members of this family are all generally long and slender, and they have no internal lungs. That is why they appear to be slim to us. Instead, they 'breathe' through their thin, moist skin. A red-backed salamander has to remain moist or it will suffocate.

Red-backed salamanders have surprisingly active lives, including elaborate courtship rituals that are conducted from

A pair of red-backed salamanders.

October to April. These animals are very tolerant of cold temperatures and may be found on warm winter days near the surface of the ground, where they continue their courtship. On colder days they retreat farther underground.

Female red-backs lay small clusters of eggs in the spring and will actually curl around the eggs protectively while they develop. When the eggs hatch, the babies appear as miniature copies of their already tiny parents. The babies then go hunting for small invertebrates during the nights and hide in the day.

At this time of year it is not too likely that you will come upon any frogs, but in the warmer months leopard frogs may patrol the edges of your woodpile, searching for insects and other invertebrates. You may also find that you have a toad that has made the woodpile pile its home. Most likely it is an American toad, and it will hide in the wood during the day, but come out at night to hunt.

Finally, there is one last group of animals that may be regular visitors to any woodpile. Snakes take advantage of the cover

An eastern garter snake tests the air.

that woodpiles provide, but they are also looking for food. All of the animals that I have mentioned, possibly with the exception of the weasel, can be prey for different kinds of snakes. The most common snake in the Northeast is the eastern garter snake. It is a relatively small snake, black with yellow stripes running the length of the body, and it will readily hunt slugs, salamanders, small frogs and toads, and insects. Larger snakes, such as corn snakes, may come to your woodpile looking for mice, voles, shrews, and chipmunks. Corn snakes are constrictors and subdue their prey by coiling their bodies around the animal and then squeezing. Their objective is not to crush the animal to death, but rather to suffocate it. Please remember that 99 percent of the snakes you see are harmless to humans, and the remaining 1 percent don't want any trouble. Don't kill them just because they are snakes.

Of course, anyone with a pile of wood that needs moving will want to see one particular variety of vertebrates that I haven't mentioned yet. These animals can be both the most enjoyable and the most irritating of all woodpile visitors, but they can also be quite helpful to you. These animals are young primates, and they may actually have had breakfast with you this morning. They are young humans, your children, and I am sure that they would just love to help you move wood today.

Just remember that they are both intelligent and fast. You should probably try to track them down before they read the signs of work to be done and make themselves scarce. Good hunting!

A black rat snake.

The Black Rat Snake

As a nature photographer, I have come to understand that two very powerful forces govern my life. These two forces act in concert to provide balance, and in much the same way that Yin and Yang are separate but almost inseparable, these two forces are rarely encountered alone. They are Nikonus and Iso, the photo gods.

Nikonus, the masculine god, is responsible for precision, timing, and luck. He can be generous to photographers who follow the 'rules.' There are many rules that photographers must abide by, but the first and foremost is this: never go anywhere without your camera. Any photographer out there knows exactly what I am speaking of. Follow the rules and Nikonus will provide you with unexpected encounters with animals that you have been searching for in vain. Fail to follow the rules, and you will be taunted with hints of birds or flowers that you cannot take pictures of, which may cause great pain.

The feminine goddess, Iso, is responsible for sensitivity, understanding, and mercy. She will soften the light on any given day if it will help a photograph look more beautiful, and she will soothe Nikonus when he is angry, possibly allowing a photographer who has broken the rules to escape the full might of a wrathful god.

Acting alone, either of these deities can be formidable, but when they act together on your behalf, the results can be spectacular. I recall one day, some years ago, when the fortune of both gods smiled down upon me. It was a wonderful day, hot and humid but not oppressive. The summer was bidding farewell to the world, and autumn was taking charge of things. I was visiting a favorite nature area and, most important of all, I had my cameras with me. I was walking down a quiet dirt road, soaking up every sound and smell that Nature had to offer, when I caught sight of a strange shape out of the corner of my eye.

At first I thought it was some kind of hose, or a piece of electrical wiring that had been left leaning against a tree, but half a second later I realized that I was looking at the largest snake I had ever seen! Even though I could plainly see that it was a snake, it still took a moment for the sight to properly register on my brain.

The snake was absolutely beautiful, and fortunately for me it had observed my approach and had frozen in place in an attempt to hide from notice. This meant that if I approached it slowly, I would be able to get a much better look at it, which I obviously did. Was this the work of innate survival instincts honed over millions of years, or was it proof of the gods' benevolent nature? Had Nikonus orchestrated the timing of the meeting, and Iso ensured that the lighting was perfect? There can be no doubt about it!

As I stood there gazing at the magnificence of the animal, I started to sort through everything I knew about snakes. I knew, for instance, that there were only two species of large black snakes that could be found in the area where we were hiking. One was the northern black racer *(Coluber constrictor constrictor)*, and the other was the black rat snake *(Elaphe obsoleta obsoleta)*. Just in case you are wondering, snakes have a tendency to hybridize quite readily, which means three-parted scientific names are often needed to accurately identify which particular snake you are talking about.

Identifying the snake was not a problem once it decided to freeze in place. The black racer, as its name suggests, is a very fast snake. What its name doesn't say is that the black racer is quick to flee when approached. The rat snake, on the other hand, is well known for freezing in place, presumably in the hope that it will be overlooked. So, these two large, black snakes can easily be identified just on behavior alone.

And they are large too. The black racer can grow to five feet long, but the rat snake can grow to six feet long. The record for the longest black rat snake ever recorded is an astonishing 8½ feet! The individual I ran into was probably in the neighborhood of 4 feet or so.

Black rat snakes are particularly interesting because of their affinity for deep forest habitat. Snakes don't usually seek out such forests, but black rat snakes have adapted to the habitat very nicely. Their long, slender bodies help them to climb into trees, where they may spend days at a time hiding in the branches or in high hollows. Their chief foods, however, bring them down to earth.

Adult rat snakes usually feed on small mammals, consuming mice, voles, chipmunks, shrews, and even fully grown squirrels. They will also eat bird eggs, which they encounter while up in trees. Younger rat snakes focus most of their attention on frogs, but they will also eat small mice if they can catch them. All of their prey is wrapped in coils and constricted before eaten.

If a rat snake happens to live near a farm, it may take advantage of the setting to hunt rats (this is presumably how the species got its name). Unfortunately, many rat snakes meet an untimely end when encountered by humans. A big black snake can be very intimidating on its own, but the rat snake also has the habit of vibrating its tail if it is cornered. This gives it an uncanny resemblance to a rattlesnake (which is exactly what it tries to give itself, no doubt), but it also may scare people enough to reach for a shovel.

Black rat snakes are completely harmless to humans, however. In fact, a big snake that eats rats may actually sound pretty nice to anyone who has a rat problem. So if you ever see a big black snake, just take the time to look at it carefully. There simply isn't any good reason to kill a snake when there are so many other options, chief among them being that of just walking away with no harm done to either party.

Black rat snakes usually emerge from their dens in the spring, which is also when they breed. Females will lay up to fifteen eggs in rotten logs in midsummer, which gives the youngsters a chance to hatch and find a place to hibernate before the winter arrives. Adults typically find deep rocky dens to spend the winter in, which they may share with many other species of snakes. Such dens are very valuable and will be used year after year by many individuals.

The black rat snake is on the endangered or threatened lists of many states in the Northeast. It may be illegal to harass, kill, or possess a rat snake, but many collectors ignore such rules and take them from the wild to sell as pets. I don't want to be part of the problem, so I won't tell anyone where I met up with this beautiful creature. I would much rather know that it is living its peaceful life, climbing trees and basking in the sun on cool mornings, without any interference from people.

For me, the encounter was nothing less than a titanic victory in its purest form, but I probably shouldn't try to take all of the credit. It is true that I decided to go for a walk, and it is also true that I remembered to bring my cameras. I walked for hours that day, and the weight of the equipment I was carrying could have easily caused me to turn back at every step. But I didn't. I forged ahead, keeping my eyes open and constantly scanning the landscape before me, and it just may be possible that I was rewarded for my efforts by the gods themselves.

Asters

September provides the perfect conditions for misty mornings, and it seems as though all of the animals respond to them. I recall one year when I visited Greylock Glen in the Berkshires of Massachusetts when this seemed to be particularly true. The fog was thick in the sheltered bowl, filled with beaver ponds and other wetlands, and all of the animals seemed to be out and about.

Gray catbirds, still hanging around until it got a little colder, called their whiny catbird calls from the thickets. Blue jays were everywhere, and a family of crows, hidden in the tops of trees that were totally obscured by thick mist, seemed to be having a lengthy conversation about who knows what. I saw a red fox cross the road, and there were rabbits everywhere (presumably what had attracted the attention of the fox).

As the sun slowly rose and started to burn its way through the mist, I almost expected to see Frodo Baggins and his band of adventurers come walking out of the fog. I didn't end up seeing him, but I did find myself in the middle of a landscape awash with color. Most of these colors were greens and yellows—fairly typical stuff for September—but here and there I caught sight of the telltale reds of the coming autumn.

I was also treated to the blues and purples of Nature's last great offering of flowers for the season—the asters. Now I must definitely mention that a great deal of the yellow in the land-scape was produced by goldenrod flowers, but so many trees also turn yellow that it is not as remarkable as the color purple. Only flowers create bright, vivacious purple.

That is about the only easy thing about asters. They are beautiful flowers to be sure, but they are just as confusing as they are beautiful, and that can mean trouble for anyone who tries to identify them.

Why all of the confusion? Well, if you look through any decent wildflower guide, you will find more than forty species listed under the heading *aster*. My *Newcomb's Wildflower Guide* lists forty-three. My *Peterson Field Guide to Wildflowers of Northeastern/Northcentral North America* lists forty-four species. And my *Illustrated Flora of the Northern United States and Canada*, by Britton and Brown (this is an awesome book), lists seventy-five species in the aster genus, which is particularly confusing because there are also 123 common names listed in the aster section of the index.

The confusion is further exacerbated when you start looking at the text. I find the calico aster (*Aster lateriflorus*) listed in the white aster section of one book, but the description of the flowers goes something like this: "Several small flower heads of white or pale purple ray flowers surrounding yellow or purple disc flowers . . ." So, if you ever find yourself frustrated by this group . . . join the crowd. I can feel your pain.

Nevertheless, asters are beautiful. Not just pretty, they are beautiful, and you shouldn't let a little confusion prevent you from enjoying these wonderful additions to the landscape of early autumn. To help ease your pain just a little, I thought I would introduce you to a few of the easier species to know.

In my opinion, the most beautiful of all the asters is the New England aster (*Aster novae-angliae*). Perched atop stems that can grow 2 to 8 feet in height, the flowers of the New England aster can be up to 2 inches in diameter (about as big as any aster flowers ever get.) Each flower is composed of forty to fifty rays that circle the center of the flower in a flat plane.

This is the standard design for aster flowers, but what makes the New England aster stand out from the others is the color. Whereas most of the colored asters are either pale blue or purple, New England asters are a deep, rich, royal purple. This color, combined with the golden yellow of the central disc, is stunning. These flowers bloom from August to October and can very easily be observed from your car. Just take the time to look for them, and you will be surprised by how many you see.

Next comes the New York aster (*Aster novi-belgii*). The flowers of the New York aster are similar in size and shape to those of the New England, but they are a pale, bluish lavender. In addition, there are generally more flowers on an individual New York aster plant, and they tend to be spread around more than those of the New England, which occur mostly at the tops of the plant stems.

Both species grow in similar areas. One of my books lists the habitat of New England asters as wet thickets, meadows,

New England aster.

and swamps, whereas the New York aster prefers shores, damp thickets, and meadows. What is the difference between a wet thicket and a damp thicket? Please ask someone else.

Once you get away from the remarkably dark color of the New England aster, you start to get into trouble. There is another species, the purple-stemmed aster, which looks remarkably similar to the New York aster. There are definitely differences, but they are smaller and harder to figure out for beginners. Purple-stemmed asters grow in swamps and low thickets, but so can New York asters. See how things can get confusing?

So why don't I move on to another easy species—the white wood aster (*Aster divaricatus*)? The white wood aster may be one

New England asters

of the most abundant asters across the autumn landscape, and to make things even easier, these plants tend to live in the woods. As a result, the plants have to produce more foliage to support themselves in the shaded habitat. Each plant can produce only a few flowers, but there can be so many plants out there, they can turn the floor of the autumn forest white in places.

Could it really be this easy? Unfortunately, the answer is no. It turns out that there are two or three different species of white asters that live in the woods. What you may originally identify as a white wood aster might, after careful scrutiny, actually be a whorled aster (*Aster acuminatus*), based on the configuration of the plant's leaves. Also known as whorled wood aster and mountain aster, the rays (petals) of these flowers are a little longer than those of white wood asters. So, you can very plainly see that both species are "white wood asters," but both species are not white wood asters . . . if you see what I mean.

Well, I have a headache. My suggestion is this: get yourself outside and enjoy the gorgeous mornings that late September and early October are going to provide for you. True, it can be hard to get up at dawn, but dawn is coming later and later each morning.

Bring a cup of something warm to sip, find yourself a quiet country road, and go for a walk. If you like a challenge, get yourself a field guide to flowers (preferably illustrated in color) and try to identify any asters you see. Some will be easy and others will be tricky, but all are beautiful and worth seeing. All it takes is a little practice, and you may find that you have a knack for identifying asters.

Dragonflies

They usually announce themselves with a rattle of dry wings. Most often associated with lakes, ponds, and rivers, they can actually be found almost anywhere if you look closely enough. They are bright, they are colorful, and they are fast. What am I describing? Dragonflies!

Though they are active during most of the warm months of the year, fall is the season for dragonfly watching. You'll have to act quickly if you want to see them, however, because the falling temperatures of autumn spell trouble for adult dragonflies. So head out to a pond, sit yourself down, and this is what you might see.

Midday is the best time to go dragonfly hunting because it is the time when males are most likely to be patrolling their territories. During the rest of the day, dragonflies head into fields and forests to hunt other flying insects. The largest dragonflies can tackle fairly large insects, but all dragonflies are particularly fond of mosquitoes!

There's no telling which species of dragonfly you might encounter at any given spot (there are 420 species that can be found in the United States alone, 4,870 worldwide), but they all have a fairly similar lifestyle. As a result, I can give you an example by focusing on one of our most easily identifiable species—the twelve-spot skimmer (*Libellula pulchella*).

The male twelve-spot skimmer is a magnificent dragonfly! From head to tail the body measures in at 2½ inches, and the beautiful wings of this dragonfly can measure up to 3⅛ inches across. The insect's name is derived from the twelve black spots that decorate its wings (three spots on each of the four wings.)

Males can be identified by the presence of milky white panels between the black spots, but the females do not have this characteristic. As a result, a female twelve-spot skimmer looks almost identical to another female dragonfly in our area, the female white tail (*Plathemis lydia*).

As it happens, however, female dragonflies are not as easily observed as the males, and since both the twelve-spot skimmer and the white tail inhabit the same basic habitats, the identification of females is most easily done by watching the behavior of males.

Male dragonflies are very territorial. Each male will do his best to stake out a portion of a pond, marsh, or slow-moving

A male twelve-spotted skimmer.

stream in the hope that a female of his species will happen by. To claim his territory, a male dragonfly will select three to four exposed perches from which he will stand guard.

Dragonflies are predatory insects, and they have huge eyes that allow them to survey much of the airspace around them. They can even turn and swivel their heads, which allows them to scan a broader section of their turf from one location. Very little escapes their attention.

As soon as a male twelve-spot skimmer catches sight of another male, the chase is on! He may simply head out to escort his rival off his territory, but he may also lock into physical combat with his opponent. Facing each other, with legs locked, two male dragonflies fighting look something like sumo wrestlers, though I have to say that dragonflies are just a bit more graceful.

A ruby meadowhawk.

It is this territorial behavior of the males that is so easy to observe. You can even introduce a new lookout tower by anchoring a nice dead stick into the mud at the margin of a pond. Sit quietly next to the stick and eventually the resident male dragonfly will come over to investigate. This is exactly how I was able to get the photograph of the twelve-spot skimmer featured with this article. I just put a stick in front of me, focused my camera, and waited. It took only about five minutes before the local champion showed up.

When a female dragonfly does finally appear, the males will get very excited and become easily agitated. All they can do is protect their territories, however, because the female appears to make the final choice. Once she makes her selection, mating takes place.

This is another aspect of the dragonfly life cycle that is easy to observe, and quite fascinating too. Just prior to mating, the male dragonfly deposits sperm cells (which are produced at the tip of the abdomen) onto a structure on the ventral side of the thorax, near the hind legs. This structure is analogous to a penis.

When the male and female join, the male grasps the female just behind the head with special claspers on the end of his abdomen. At the same time the female arches her abdomen under her own body so she can reach the structure on the male's thorax where the sperm has been deposited. Two dragonflies locked in this position are almost impossible to miss.

Once mating has been successfully completed, the male and female part. The male may go back to his perches to look for another female, but the female has to set about the business of laying her eggs. She does this by hovering over the pond and dipping her abdomen into the water over and over and over. This is another behavior that is easy to observe.

When the eggs hatch, the nymphs start their lives as predators. They patrol the muddy bottoms of lakes, ponds, and slow streams by walking on their fully developed legs (they are insects, so they have three pairs of legs), and when they spot a smaller animal, they attack with their special jaws.

Located at the end of a special hinged structure called a *labium*, the jaws of a dragonfly nymph are very sharp. When not in use, the labium is folded under the head, but in a flash the labium can be extended up to one-third of the nymph's body length, sort of like a chameleon's tongue.

When in danger, the dragonfly nymph can escape by using jet power. It can take in a huge amount of water through its mouth, fill up its abdomen (its tail), and then squeeze the water out of its abdomen with great force. The result is a jet-powered burst of speed that can carry the nymph to safety.

As you sit by a pond and watch for dragonflies, you may also notice some of their smaller, but no less interesting relatives, the damselflies. The best way to differentiate between dragonflies and damselflies is by looking at the way they hold their wings. Dragonfly wings are held out perpendicular to the body like the wings of an airplane. Damselflies, on the other hand, fold their wings in line with their bodies while at rest. Despite this small physiological difference, dragonflies and damselflies have very similar life cycles.

Adult dragonflies (and damselflies) have no escape from the cold and die when the weather changes. The nymphs survive the winter at the bottoms of ponds and will emerge as adults the following year, but they are not as easy to observe as the graceful adults that crisscross the placid surfaces of ponds on lazy autumn days. They are out there right now; all you have to do is go and find them.

Katydids

Autumn is a strange season. Typically we think of autumn as being those few short weeks when the leaves start to change color and the birds start to abandon the north for more favorable conditions in the south. It is a time of getting back to school and trying to forget the freedom of summer.

For many of us it may feel as though autumn ends when the final leaves have fallen from the trees, but technically, autumn does not end until just three days before Christmas. As a result, autumn is a season with many different feels to it. Late September is surely very different from early December, so when I speak of autumn, I have to be very careful. In my mind, the feeling of autumn is best exemplified by the month of October.

Some of October can be cold and quite inclement, but other days can be surprisingly delightful. In particular I am speaking of those unexpected nights when echoes of summer seem to come reverberating out of the past. These are the hot, humid, sticky nights that are the favorites of moths that I have spoken of earlier, but other nocturnal insects may also arrive, and there may seem to be millions swarming around your porch light.

These nights are also filled with sounds! Crickets are probably the most iconic of the nighttime insects, and the different songs of the various species can lend a certain comfortable feeling to an evening that is easy to recognize but hard to describe. Crickets are not the only nocturnal songsters in the insect world, however; their close relatives the katydids can sing songs that rival anything a cricket can dish out. The only difference is that not all katydid sounds are as recognizable as those of crickets are.

I can remember one such autumn evening very clearly as I sit here and write this book. I was sitting at my kitchen table at something close to midnight and listening to the chorus of insects outside when I suddenly heard something that filled my mind with the feeling of opportunity. I knew this sound viscerally, as a parent knows the sound of its own child's voice. The only question was could I convert the feeling of opportunity into real opportunity.

An oblong-winged katydid.

I got up from the table quickly, walked over to the screen door, and went out onto the porch, where I instantly found myself in a cloud of swarming little bodies. I turned to the left, toward the window over my kitchen sink, and there in the gloom I saw exactly what I was hoping for. It was a large, green insect, and as I stood there watching, I heard the unmistakable song of a katydid.

After a brief moment of silent exultation (and a quick but sincere offering of thanks to Nikonus and Iso), I sprang into action with a set of skills that I must have learned as an 8-year-old. I headed back to the kitchen in search of a container. When I was a kid, I always looked for one of the ubiquitous canning jars that filled my mother's kitchen and pantry, or possibly a metal coffee can that still had its lid. This night, however, I had to settle for a large plastic yogurt container, which was actually perfect for the job.

I went back outside with fingers crossed, saw to my delight that the katydid was still there and still singing, cautiously approached the beautiful insect, and then carefully . . . oh so carefully . . . captured it without harming it. Success!! I had my subject and now had only to wait until morning. So I gingerly poked a couple of holes in the lid of the container, placed it on its side on the kitchen windowsill, and went back to my reading.

After the initial shock of being captured, the katydid even relaxed enough to rejoin the nighttime chorus, answering other katydids outside. It was a genuinely pleasurable moment for me and reminded me of the long, lazy summers of my childhood, when summer nights were spent in pursuit of fireflies and frogs, all of which spent a single night in a jar by my bedside before being set free the next morning.

So I have a little secret to share with you: youth is a state of mind! Turn off the TV, grab a metal coffee can, a canning jar, or a yogurt container, go outside, and see if you can capture a moth, a beetle, or a frog, and a nostalgic slice of your childhood. It's really fun!

Anyway, the incredible humidity of that night gave way to a spectacular morning. The sky was blue, the temperature had fallen back down to something 'normal' for autumn, and it was truly nice to be outside. I took a careful look in the yogurt container and found myself being placidly regarded by the katydid. So I got my cameras ready, went outside, crossed my fingers, and opened the lid of the container. Fortune smiled upon me once again, and the katydid came out cautiously. I placed the katydid on the porch railing, and it took a moment to collect its bearings. Then it leapt into the air and flew to a patch of tall weeds at the edge of my flower garden. There it landed on a chicory plant, where it stayed for a while, eating flower petals and cleaning itself in the fastidious manner that all insects share.

Something about katydids that few people realize is the amazing number of species that can be found worldwide. Care to make a guess? Well, if your guess was somewhere around 4 thousand species, you were correct. Of the 4 thousand species, a full half can be found in the Amazon. North of the Mexican border we have just over 200 species.

Katydids are members of the same family of insects as the grasshoppers and crickets, and of the two they are more closely related to crickets. Like their smaller, chirping cousins, katydids are nocturnal. Unlike most crickets, however, katydids are arboreal, which means they have an affinity for trees. It is for this reason that many species of katydids have gone to such extreme lengths to mimic leaves as closely as possible. Some species have even gone so far as to include brown spots in their disguise, to mimic dead parts of leaves.

The katydid I captured turned out to be a member of the false katydid genus, and I identified it as an oblong-winged katydid (*Amblycorypha oblongifolia*). If you live in an area that has mature oak trees, you may be more familiar with the songs of the common true katydid (*Pterophylla camellifolia*), which has the distinctive three-part song that very loudly proclaims, "Kay-tee-did, kay-tee-didn't, kay-tee-did, kay-tee-didn't."

Oblong-winged kaytdids have a song much more reminiscent of a cricket song, only imagine the cricket singing very loudly with laryngitis and you've got the idea. Unlike crickets, katydids sing at intervals and seem to produce much more volume. This could possibly be a result of their much larger wings, which produce their songs when rubbed together.

The katydid I captured also turned out to be a male. This may have been obvious since it was his singing that alerted me to his presence, but the lack of an ovipositor was also a good clue. An ovipositor is a tube through which females lay their eggs. A female's ovipositor is quite obvious where it emerges from the end of the abdomen, and this individual was clearly lacking one.

So, enjoy the songs of the katydids while they last. They will continue singing every night, but their songs will slow down noticeably as the temperatures steadily drop. They will not give up until the frost gets them, and then the silence of the coming winter will once again cover the land. Until that fateful night arrives, however, you should be sure to keep a yogurt container handy and head outside to see what wonders lie hidden in the dark of an autumn night.

Slabsides

For many years now I have been working as a science teacher at Pittsfield High School in Pittsfield, Massachusetts. As a result, every September I am reined in from the freedom of summer along with all of my students, and outdoor time starts to become a precious commodity. Gone are the pleasant summer evenings of staying up to watch for satellites on any night of my choosing. In September my nature forays are limited to the weekends.

Needless to say, this has been a big change for me. Before working as a teacher, I worked in various jobs that were much more closely tied to Nature and the outdoors. In the late 1990s and early "oughts" I worked as a naturalist for the Massachusetts State Parks. I was able to spend hours outside—surrounded by peace and quiet—and to immerse myself in whatever season was unfolding at the moment.

As a teacher, however, I am forced to spend a lot of time looking at Nature through windows. As the days shorten and the season shifts from late summer to early autumn, I can start to feel as though I'm missing out on everything altogether. I get up when it's still dark out and leave for work before the horizon is light. Some days I am lucky to leave work before the sun goes down, but I have found driving past Nature to be wholly unsatisfying. After six weeks of this routine I need a break.

As a first-year teacher, I settled upon an acceptable antidote that has turned into a pleasant annual ritual. If I want to take a soul-restoring soak in a pool of autumn's beauty, I simply block off a weekend in early October, jump into my jeep with my wife, and make a pilgrimage to Slabsides.

In 1874 John Burroughs (my favorite nature writer) moved into a large house on the western shore of the Hudson River that Burroughs named Riverby. It was a large house and served as his permanent home for the rest of his life, but after twenty years of living by the river, Burroughs tired of his surroundings. He wrote:

> To a countryman like myself, not born to a great river or an extensive water view, these things, I think, become wearisome after a time. Scenery may be too fine or too grand and imposing for one's hourly view. Hence, it is never wise to build your house on the most ambitious spot in the landscape. Rather, seek out a more humble and sheltered nook or corner, which you can fill and warm with domestic and home instincts and affections. In some things the half is more satisfying than the whole.

In 1895, when he was presented with the opportunity to purchase just such a nook a few miles from Riverby, Burroughs pounced. He purchased a 20-acre tract well away from the Hudson and built a rustic cabin that he named Slabsides because its outer walls were covered with slabs (the first bark-covered planks cut from trees when making lumber).

Fortunately for all of us, Slabsides was recognized as an important landmark and is now the main attraction of the 170-acre John Burroughs Sanctuary. I still remember my first visit to this wonderful spot. It would be a long journey, but I felt a trip to Slabsides was just what I needed.

I got up early on a rainy day and headed for the town of West Park in the Catskills. It was cold and quite windy out, but my drive down the Hudson was a rather pleasant one. The areas I drove through gave me a hint of what Burroughs might have been running from as this region has the look of being some-what rundown.

Before my visit I had difficulty coming to grips with Bur-roughs' ability to write so passionately about Nature, but then I turned off the main roads and headed away from the Hudson River on Floyd Ackert Road. In just moments I was transported into the mountains, and as I approached the entrance to the sanctuary, I was greeted by two mother turkeys with their nine babies. It was as if Burroughs had known I was coming and decided to roll out a red carpet.

The rain was falling steadily when I finally parked my car and headed down an old dirt road, but the chill of the day didn't seem to bother me. I was far too excited and had completely fallen under the spell of the mist that was drifting through the hemlocks that lined the road. The way was mysterious, and I constantly looked into the gloom for hints of what lay ahead.

And then there it was. It took me by surprise at first because the entire building is sided in bark. It blended in perfectly, and the fog sufficiently hid its roofline so there was no tremendously obvious angle to see. It seemed almost to materialize out of no-

Burroughs' beloved "Slabsides."

where, and its appearance made for a wonderful greeting to a place that meant so much to me.

Burroughs built Slabsides with trees in their raw, just-cut form wherever possible. The mantelpiece around his fireplace is was made of young yellow birches that were put into place with their bark still on, and the pilings for his front porch were simply white pines that had been cut to fit.

As I climbed the stairs of his porch and sat down in the same spot where a photograph of Burroughs and his granddaughter had been taken, I felt the stress of my day-to-day life being replaced with the calm and peace of a rainy day in the mountains. I would have paid almost anything to smell the sweet perfume of a wood fire, but I had to try to imagine it as best I could.

After a time I headed off to visit a small lake in the sanctuary, and I was delighted to find one of the most beautiful scenes to ever fall upon my eyes. A rocky island covered with pines and young sassafras trees was surrounded by water covered with rain-drop rings and steaming in the cool air. I just walked silently, holding Susan's hand and taking pictures whenever I could. It was a wonderful day.

And this is something that I would suggest that you do for yourself too. You don't have to go to Slabsides, but you should take the time to go somewhere quiet so you can unwind. We work very hard in this world we have created, and we have surrounded ourselves with noise, fluorescent lights, and the smell of chemicals. It is important for each of us to get away from these factors every now and again in order to remind ourselves of what is important in life.

Bring a friend or a loved one, hold hands or talk quietly, or just wander off into the unknown by yourself with a cheerful whistle if you prefer, but do something. I always feel the positive effects of my own trips in the weeks that follow, and I will always know that I can do it again should the need arise.

Nature's Pantry

The Earth lies some 93 million miles from the sun. To make a complete orbit of the sun in one year, the Earth must travel at a constant speed of roughly 67,000 miles per hour. None of us feels as though we are moving that fast, but there is very good evidence that it is happening for anyone who pays attention to the right sorts of things.

In addition to moving so quickly, the Earth is also tilted a little, relative to the sun. As the Earth moves around the sun in its orbit, the tilt remains constant, which means that different parts of the planet are pointed toward the sun at different times of year. The consequences of this tilt are most pronounced in the polar areas, and least conspicuous in the equatorial regions.

This is all very abstract when seen on paper, but there is hard evidence of this process right outside our windows for all of us to observe and contemplate. Each day the Earth travels about 1.6 million miles in its orbit, and as winter approaches, this means the Northern Hemisphere is swinging farther and farther away from the sun. This process happens quickly in November and can result in a decrease of three to four minutes of daylight every day.

We recognize the effects of this change in basic, everyday terms. The decreasing light levels trigger a change in the color of tree leaves, and soon after they will fall to the ground. The trees start to go into a period of dormancy, and the birds that once filled the forests and ate the insects that fed on the tree leaves will flee to the south.

It also starts to get colder. A couple of consecutive nights with a hard frost signal the approach of winter, and you may even see thin sheets of ice forming in the birdbath overnight. Soon after, even the hardiest crickets will fall victim to the cold, and a great silence will settle over the landscape. We will all feel it in our bones, and we all know it is true—winter is coming.

For many of us, this means a comfortable and pleasant series of winter preparations must be seen to. We must put away the window screens and replace them with storm windows. Dusty corners of garages must be swept out to make way for stacks of folding chairs. Flowerpots must be emptied and sorted.

The nuts of a shagbark hickory are an example of "hard mast."

Snow blowers must be brought out, tuned up, and tested. Basically, everyone will start battening down the hatches. For many of my friends, this also seems to require a last mowing of the lawn, and I too have this compulsion. I may even go out and give it one final run around the house, but I make sure not to get carried away. I always try to remember those animals that seem to live at the mercy of the weather. While I can stack firewood and fill up my pantry with canned goods and dry goods galore, there are many birds that seem to live quite risky lives of luck and chance.

These little creatures cannot store up food for the winter and must rely instead on waking up every morning and going out to find food. They rely on Nature's pantry to provide for their needs, and when the last of the leaves fall from the trees, the pantry is as full as it's going to be. What is so very interesting to me is how human activities can impact the amount of food the pantry holds.

This idea was exemplified one year when I was getting the area around my woodpile ready for the sorting and stacking of firewood that were soon to commence. I caught a movement out of the corner of my eye, and there was a little goldfinch foraging for chicory seeds in an area of lawn that I hadn't mowed.

After that encounter I paid a lot of attention to my yard, and I was quite pleased to see many birds quietly hunting and picking through the tall grasses that I left uncut. It made me happy to know that I, in my own way, had provided food for the goldfinch by simply not obsessive-compulsively cutting every square inch of my yard to within two inches of the ground.

Thus, I am always a little saddened when I see my neighbors following their own compulsions to mow fields that had gone without a single cutting all summer. There can be so much food ready and waiting for the birds, but the mowers will render the seeds largely useless as soon as the first snow falls. I realize that some fields need to be cut occasionally, but others can be left uncut for several years before the brush needs to be mowed back.

In addition to the seeds that can be found in fields, there are also great quantities of food that can be found in and around the forested areas of the landscape. Wildlife biologists often refer to these foods as *mast*, and mast comes in two basic types. *Hard mast* basically refers to tree nuts and large seeds. The most easily recognized examples of hard mast would probably be acorns, but would also include beechnuts, walnuts, hickory nuts, and even pine, maple, and ash seeds. These are rather sturdy, hard, long-lasting seeds that are meant to survive the winter and sprout as young trees in the spring.

There is another category of food known as *soft mast*. Grapes, apples, berries, and other soft fruits that contain seeds but do not have hard shells fall into this group. Some kinds of soft mast (such as blackberries and raspberries) have very short shelf lives, whereas others can linger on through most of the winter (the waxy, white berries of poison ivy are a great example).

Taken together, the nuts, acorns, seeds, and berries represent all of the food there is going to be for the rest of the fall, the winter, and the early part of spring. Birds such as song sparrows will hunker down in one spot and try to eke out a living by carefully exploring their territories and exploiting every possible source of food that can be found.

For the sparrows and finches, each stem of long grass, Queen Anne's lace, and smartweed left standing is available food. Anything mowed is lost. For other birds such as cedar waxwings, winter is an endless search for food that may take the birds on great journeys. Waxwings look for soft mast such as cedar berries and crab apples, and they have to keep moving as they eat their way across the landscape.

Then there are the forest birds, such as wild turkeys, that have to wander through the woods and pick up fallen grapes, acorns, and anything else that is edible. Eating and putting on weight are very important for turkeys, because as the snow gets deeper and deeper, their access to food is greatly curtailed. Winters with prolonged periods of very deep snow can be disastrous for turkeys.

So from now until spring, every day that passes means there is less and less food for the animals that have remained. They have no ability to influence the amount of food available, and many do not have the ability to store food, so they are literally at the mercy of Nature. If it was a good year for seeds, they will do well. If it was a poor year for seeds, however, the winter may not be so kind.

If you can resist the human urge to cut, flatten, and 'clean,' then you may be able to add just a little more food to the larder. It may not feel as though you are doing much, but you can always hack away at the weeds in the spring AFTER all of the animals have had a chance to eat that one more meal that you provided.

An American goldfinch feeds in tall weeds that we left unmowed.

WINTER

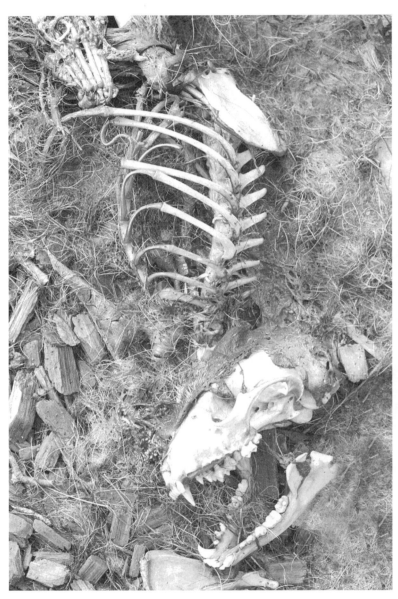

A raccoon skeleton.

Endurance

On December 27, 1831, a young naturalist named Charles Darwin set sail on a journey that would take him around the world and into history. The HMS Beagle, under the command of Captain Robert Fitz-Roy, was charged with surveying the coast of Patagonia and producing coastal maps, harbor plans, and hydrological charts for the British admiralty. Darwin's part in this endeavor was twofold.

First and foremost, he was to serve as a companion to Fitz-Roy. The voyage of the Beagle would be a long one, and the captain knew he needed someone to talk with who was definitely not a regular member of the crew. Darwin had been educated at Edinburgh University to become a physician, and later at Cambridge to become a clergyman, so he was well prepared for long discussions on varying subjects. Though Fitz-Roy was often unpredictable, the two managed to get along fairly well.

The second of Darwin's responsibilities (and the more important from the view of science and history) was to serve as the ship's naturalist. Today, naturalists are sometimes thought of as friendly people who take others on walks to see birds or flowers. In truth, however, naturalists are much, much more. They are people who have studied broadly, who understand many disciplines of science at many different levels, and can bring them together in such a manner that the layman can make sense of them.

In Darwin's day the role of naturalist was highly respected. Generally speaking, it was only men of great wealth who had the opportunity to acquire all of the necessary education to be effective in such a vocation. Fortunately (for all of us) Darwin was a born naturalist. His affinity for all forms of nature, but particularly for beetles, led in part to his rather lackluster performance at both Edinburgh and Cambridge. In his autobiography he wrote, ". . . no pursuit at Cambridge was followed with so much eagerness or gave me so much pleasure as collecting beetles."

Darwin was very lucky to get to do the one thing he most wanted to, and the human race is still collecting the dividends of his ideas. To my mind, the most important of his ideas is "the survival of the fittest." Put quite simply, more organisms are born than can possibly survive. All of these organisms have slight variations in their bodies that give them certain advantages over others.

To survive, the organisms have to compete with one another over limited resources, and this competition is always unfair. The environment will present certain conditions for the organisms to deal with, and only the ones with the advantages are going to survive. In biology, fitness is defined as the ability to survive and procreate. Thus, the survivors—the ones with all of the advantages—are the fittest.

Now this may seem familiar to some of you, but you may not realize that this sort of thing is going on all day . . . every day . . . right in your back yard. Every single plant, animal, fungus, protozoan, and bacterium that lives within sight of your back window is struggling to deal with whatever nature dishes up. For all of these organisms, losing the challenge means losing life itself.

My own back yard offers up hints of this struggle no matter what the season may be. In the winter, I might walk down the trail through my field and find deer tracks in the snow. Often they are stained brown by the muddy meltwater that the warmer temperatures have allowed to accumulate under the crusty white surface. There may even be a spot where I can see the streaks in the snow left by sodden hooves dripping mud on the snow.

Tracks such as these are usually rather fresh and serve as proof that at least one of the neighborhood deer has survived the winter. I don't have the skills required to tell if the deer is healthy, or on the verge of death. All I know is that this particular deer walked through my yard and is still in the game. Where will that deer be by the time you read this? It's impossible to say.

Every spring I am impressed by the number of feather piles in the long line of white pines that border the western edge of my yard. This evidence of the dangerous game between predator and prey shows that there is at least one raptor that is regularly successful in picking off some of the doves that visit my feeders. I rarely see such an attack take place, but I often see the hawks patrolling the thickets and fields surrounding my house, and the alertness of the smaller birds is proof that the hawks are a routine threat.

What really surprised me one year was the evidence of a different kind of struggle that I found at a bend in my trail through the pines. Perched atop the crusty snow was part of the wing of a raptor. To me, the feathers were small enough to suggest they belonged to a sharp-shinned hawk. What was truly fascinating about the discovery was the fact that it put the struggle for survival into perspective.

We often think of predators moving through the landscape and picking off the old, or the infirm. But what we often fail to realize is that even the predators can be become sick or injured. Furthermore, if the predator isn't particularly large, it may have predators of its own that it has to watch out for. I have no idea what killed the hawk. I only know that it lost the fight for survival in some way or another.

And let's not forget the rather miserable addition of winter rain and ice that we all have to endure from time to time. Many trees lose limbs as a result of the added weight of the ice, and some may end up dying as a result. Pine trees are often able to shed unwanted snow off their limbs, but the odd growth patterns resulting from pine weevil damage can put limbs at risk. Other pines around the most heavily affected trees may weather the storms with minimal damage, but heavily "weeviled" trees may take a lot of damage. Will rot set in and eventually kill the tree? Even trees struggle to survive.

Now try to put yourself into the mix. What do you think life would be like if you weren't allowed to go inside? Cold weather always gets me thinking of questions like that. I'll be sitting at my desk or lying in bed at night and listening to the wind, and I'll wonder what it must be like to have to live outside. Quite frankly, I can't really imagine it.

Humans are a curious species. Through a sequence of key evolutionary turns we have become the current masters of this planet, but in truth we are little more than a group of tropical primates that have learned a few tricks. When the temperature drops below zero, our heritage becomes painfully apparent, however. I played a lot of hockey as a kid, so I am fairly comfortable in cold weather, but my wife starts to whimper if the temperature drops much below 70. Needless to say, she spends a lot of time hiding under thick down comforters and placing orders for warm beverages during the winter months.

But what of the other animals? What do they do? The smallest animals have the most serious challenge in staying warm because of the ratio between body volume and surface area. Basically, the smaller you are, the more of you is exposed and the quicker you can lose heat. This is why researchers who study small mammals have to be careful to provide warm bedding inside live traps during research projects.

If a mouse wanders into a live trap and becomes imprisoned for an extended period of time, there is a slight risk that it will freeze to death if it doesn't have a warm nest to sleep in—and that's when it's warm out! So, way back in the good old days, I can remember carrying around a big bag of cotton when I was conducting small-mammal surveys out at the Quabbin Reservoir in central Massachusetts. A handful of cotton was lovingly fashioned into a nest and placed into the back of each trap so that all of the little test subjects were safe and sound while they waited to be poked, prodded, and released.

The advantage of being small, however, is quite simple. If you are small, you can get inside things. So, while mice may be at risk because of their small size, they are also able to build nests in all sorts of nooks and crannies. Just between you and me, there are times when I expect to see little chimneys emitting thin tendrils of smoke whenever I pass a little out-of-the-way place on a winter walk. The smoke would indicate that the tiny mice and voles are all bundled up in their slippers and smoking jackets, sitting in front of cheery fireplaces and drinking tea the way Rat and Mole do in *The Wind in the Willows*. I've never found one, but I keep looking anyway. Just don't tell anyone, or people will start to think I've gone 'round the bend.

Other mammals have hiding places sheltered from wind and rain. Foxes and coyotes have their dens, as do the skunks, woodchucks, and chipmunks that sleep through the winter. Weasels have dens, and raccoons and porcupines usually find places to live in old trees. Of all of the winter lodgings, though, the most creative would have to belong to muskrats and beavers.

These animals play a pretty dangerous game with the cold. Both species build lodges out of vegetation, the muskrat out of

At some point a small mammal tunneled up from the grass and skittered out across the snow.

cattails and the beaver out of trees. Inside these lodgings they are safe from the worst of the cold, but there is one important problem—their food is outside. Thus, it is very important that the underwater entrances to these little houses be sufficiently deep to allow access to their underwater stores of food. I'm quite sure that many a young, inexperienced beaver has paid the ultimate price for building a shallow entrance in a shallow pond, and a prolonged cold spell may be just the kind of weather that will make, or break, a beaver's future.

Birds also have their challenges, and suffer the same kinds of problems that mammals do. Very small birds play a delicate balancing act during cold weather. They have to get out to find food—enough to get them through to the next day—but they cannot expend too much energy finding it.

Thus, chickadees spend the entirety of a cold winter on the verge of starvation. Fortunately, they can climb into nighttime nests inside trees to stay warm. Most of our tiny wintertime birds do this at night, and most of them owe a great debt to the woodpeckers that build so many nest holes and provide so much winter housing.

Of all our local animals I would say that I feel the most sympathy for the turkeys and the deer. If it is very cold out, these animals pretty much have to just curl up and take it. Deep snow may help the deer, because they will be able to lie down in a deep drift and find some insulation from the snow itself. Igloos work for people, right?

But the same deep snow that helps the deer will hinder the turkeys. Remember that turkeys are ground-feeding birds, and too much snow will deny them access to food. So if it's really cold with deep snow, the turkeys are in trouble; but if it's really cold and there isn't much snow at all, then the deer suffer. Can you imagine having to curl up on the ground and try to sleep when it's 5 below zero out?

I would have included the ruffed grouse in the group with deer and turkeys if I didn't know two important things about grouse: First of all, they are not restricted to ground feeding. Grouse are quite happy searching for nutritious leaf buds high in the treetops. For this reason they are immune to almost any amount of snow, but are still in trouble if there is a heavy ice storm. The second and certainly more curious trait of grouse is their ability to do something called "snow roosting." This may be a little hard to imagine at first, but just follow along. When the snow in the forest is very deep, grouse may take shelter in it, and take advantage of its insulating properties, by bombing through the woods on the wing and then plunging into the deep snow headfirst.

I've seen photographs of this in books, but still haven't been lucky enough to find an example of my own yet. This is an ingenious solution to a big problem, but one that comes with a certain amount of risk. I wonder how many grouse have plunged into deep snow only to encounter an unfortunately placed stump?

There are lots of animals I haven't mentioned, but my space is limited. I could probably write a book on adaptations to the conditions of winter weather if I tried, but I'll just leave you with this sampler for the time being.

Remember to keep your birdfeeders stocked and your own home full of wonderful treats so you can be safe and comfortable during this cold spell. And if you should happen to feel brave and go for a walk, keep your eyes peeled! I am certain that sooner or later, in some quiet corner of a quiet field, tiny wisps of smoke will betray the secret and very cozy homes of tiny animals that spend their winters reading books in front of friendly little fires.

The Dark-eyed Junco

It is often difficult to predict how winter will unfold in any given year. Sometimes the Old Man of the North has a gentle touch; allowing everyone to get tucked in and ready for a long winter slumber. Other times he arrives almost without warning, as though he were punishing us for some transgression we have long forgotten. Regardless of the timing of the arrival of permanent snow cover, however, the creatures outside have their own schedules to keep. Plumage changes, caches are hidden, dens are sealed, migrations are made—it all goes according to plan. Every year I look forward to seeing old friends around the holidays, but they are not always human friends. Sometimes they are the little winged travelers that come only a short way to visit my feeders.

Such is the case with the dark-eyed junco *(Junco hyemalis)*. Anyone who has a birdfeeder has probably seen a junco at one time or another, but you may not recognize the name I am using. In the past, the dark-eyed junco has been known as the "slate-colored junco," the "northern junco," and about 15 other names.

All of this confusion comes totally on the part of humans, however. There are juncos all across the United States, and they can vary in appearance quite dramatically. These regional differences, it was later discovered, were in appearance only.

The same thing happens with humans! People from Asia, Africa, Europe, and North America are all members of the same species of mammal. Similarly, the juncos of differing appearance are mostly from the same species of bird. I suspect that the juncos themselves have never had any doubts about who they were, so in an effort to keep things as simple as possible, I am just going to refer to these birds as juncos.

If you have a bird book handy, and you would like to see which name your particular junco is listed under, just look up the scientific name *Junco hyemalis* in the index. The genus name, *Junco*, probably comes from the Latin word *juncus*, which means "a reed" or "a rush," which is probably a reference to the color of old reeds and rushes. The species name, *hyemalis*, stems from the Latin word *hiemalis*, which means "of, or pertaining to, winter." One of the older and sweeter names for the junco is "snowbird," which is probably an old translation of the bird's scientific name.

A pair of juncos sits atop a snow drift.

As it happens, we live in an area in which juncos are present year-round. The fact remains, however, that juncos are much more noticeable in the wintertime, as many birds from Canada will come to spend the winter here.

Juncos are small birds with a body length of five to six inches. Though not particularly bright in color, juncos are actually rather elegant, in my opinion. The males are covered with dark charcoal-gray feathers on their heads, necks, backs, wings, and tails. The only exceptions are the outer tail feathers and those of the belly, all of which are white.

This plumage coloration, once described as representing "leaden skies above, snow below," is probably another reason that juncos have been called "snowbirds" in the past. Personally, I have always thought that the bodies of male juncos looked like little black Easter eggs dipped in white paint.

Female juncos have exactly the same white markings as the males, but are covered with brownish-gray feathers over the rest of their bodies. Both sexes are remarkably hard to detect in grassy or shrubby areas, and would probably go totally unnoticed if not for the occasional flashing of their white tail feathers. They are easier to spot against a blanket of fresh snow, but they can still hide remarkably well if they want to.

Why all of this sneaking around? Would it surprise you if I told you that juncos were in the habit of hiding because they nest on the ground? The nest, built primarily by the female, is usually located in a small depression next to some sort of vertical wall. This could be a large rock, a knot of exposed tree roots, or even a bank of exposed soil. At other times, however, the female may decide to build her nest in a brush pile, a thicket of blueberry bushes, or at the base of a tree. Once, I even found a junco nest in a small depression in the middle of someone's lawn.

The usual number of eggs is four, and the female alone incubates them. The babies that hatch out of them are tiny and helpless (young birds of this type are known as *altricial*.) Both parents work together to feed their babies, each of which has to be fed eight times per hour. At a minimum, the adults have to find and capture thirty-two insects every hour to keep a full nest of babies happy and healthy.

The adults dote on their babies, even going so far as to strip the wings and legs from larger insects before they are offered as food. The babies open their eyes on their second day, and are ready to fly in as little as nine days. They then spend about three weeks following their father around while their mother prepares a second nest.

Even though juncos are very subtle in color, this should in no way suggest that they don't have very interesting personal lives. In fact, quite the opposite is true, and if you have a feeder close to your house, you may actually be able to witness some very interesting behavior.

There are aggressive chases, which are part of both male-versus-male combat and male-female courtship. When there is a squabble over birdseed, you may witness another visual display known as the "tail-up display." When this happens, a junco will lower its head and raise its fanned tail. This is always an aggressive display, and may be exchanged between birds of either sex.

Juncos also have a wonderful variety of vocalizations that are relatively easy to hear if you are willing to sit outside on a calm winter day. One, called the "kew" call, is the vocal equivalent of the tail-up display, and is very easily heard at feeders. The most common junco vocalization is known as the "tsip" call. This is a very quiet, very short, and very high-pitched call used as a contact call as groups of juncos quietly forage. This lets each bird know where the others are, so that they can move around together without having to keep looking for one another.

If you would like to attract juncos to your yard, you should try putting out some black oil sunflower seed, some mixed seed with a lot of white millet in it, and even some thistle or nyger seed. Place this seed on the ground in and around bushes where the birds will have a feeling of security. And, as always, please do not put out seed if there are cats around your house.

The numbers of juncos will increase as more and more birds are pushed south by the arrival of snow in Canada. Until it starts snowing in our area, the juncos may be content with the seeds of grasses and other plants, but once the snow starts to fall, they will gladly begin to rely on well-stocked birdfeeders.

Frozen Water

My memories of winters from my childhood are dominated by images of deep blankets of snow. There was the blizzard of 1978, the blizzard of 1980, and plenty of other heavy snow events that seem to keep these memories perpetually buried under large, drifting piles of the white stuff. But today, those memories seem so strange as to be almost unbelievable.

With every passing year there seems to be less and less snow to contend with. Ice seems to be playing an increasingly dramatic role in the Northeast, but big storms that drop two to three feet of snow seem to be much less common. Perhaps this is a predictable result of growing up, since the snow banks next to the driveway do not seem so large to someone who is so much larger than he used to be, but I still can't help but feel as though there just isn't as much around these days. Still, frozen water in its various forms dominates the winter landscape, so it might be interesting to learn what makes this stuff so magically strange.

Of all the substances on Earth, very few exhibit the curious properties of water. In most substances, whether elements or compounds, the particles that form a particular substance have a predictable manner of behaving in the solid, liquid, and gaseous states. Gasses contain the most energy, and in this state there is a lot of room between the particles, so the gaseous state is the least dense.

Virtually every liquid is the middle state as far as density is concerned. In molecular compounds, intermolecular bonding takes place as temperatures (and thus energy levels) fall and the individual molecules start to coalesce into chains or even 'webs.'

There is more to it that that, but let's just keep it in relatively simple turns so I don't have to get too involved in the physical properties of matter. A liquid, we'll say, is more stable and 'sticky' than a gas, but not as stable as a solid.

Everyone can relate to the idea that solid objects are very stable. All of our tools are made of solids, and even the crust of the Earth itself is a cool, stable solid that we depend on. In this state, matter is comprised of particles that are as efficiently packed as possible. At low temperatures there are strong inter-molecular bonds between all molecules, and regular crystalline patterns start to form.

As saturated soil freezes, the pressure squeezes water up and out into curling frozen strands.

Such is the case with water, but something strange happens when the crystal lattice of water forms. Because of the arrangement of the single oxygen and double hydrogen atoms of a water molecule, it turns out that the most efficient packing pattern for solid water has more space between the molecules than water in the liquid state. So, solid water actually turns out to be less dense than liquid water.

Using your amazing powers of critical thinking (you have had your coffee this morning, haven't you?), you should now be able to understand why ice cubes float. You should also be able to understand why copper pipes and glass bottles full of water explode when they freeze. As it freezes, the water trapped inside such vessels expands and smashes its way free of its confinement.

Sometimes this property can create some very interesting effects. Consider the wet ground of a swampy forest. As temperatures drop, a skim of ice forms on the surface. As the water continues to freeze, it starts to exert pressure on the remaining water. The only escape is upward and outward, but the water forced out into the open will freeze when it hits the cold air. This sequence of events is what led to the strange ice formation that I recorded in photographs for this chapter.

Anyone should be able to see that if not for this very rare and wonderful property of water, life on Earth would be very different indeed. For instance, imagine a pond in winter and try to visualize what would happen if water behaved like most other molecules.

Nerves tense, your mind racing, you see that water, acting like other materials, would sink when it froze. Thus, lakes and ponds would freeze from the bottom up. Either that or they would stay in their liquid state until they very quickly turned solid throughout. It's actually kind of hard to imagine.

Any fish, frog, turtle, or toad living in such conditions would have to flee or perish. Plants would simply be destroyed where they were rooted, leaving the freshly melted ponds of springtime barren and devoid of life. So you can begin to see how much the winter landscape depends on the wonderfully odd properties of water.

Now let's try to bring your amazing cognitive abilities to bear on another feature of frozen water. Ice and snow actually create amazingly effective thermal barriers between the ground and the open air. Ice forms a shield that protects the water beneath from severe cold, and snow forms an even more efficient insulator for the ground.

Everyone knows that the Earth is full of liquid hot magma. The tremendous heat from the core of the planet is constantly radiating out toward the surface and helps to keep much of the Earth's crust above the freezing point of water. Even frozen ground can vary in temperature. Ice at 30 degrees Fahrenheit is much warmer than ice at minus 30 degrees Fahrenheit.

So it should take no great leap of logic to figure out that a nice blanket of fresh, fluffy snow can serve as an outstanding insulator. The air pockets between individual snowflakes, or grains of ice, trap heat and do not allow it to be conducted out into the atmosphere. Thus, it is quite possible for the temperature at the ground-snow barrier to be as many as 30 degrees warmer than the temperature at the snow-air interface. This is nothing but good news for any little animal that lives under the snow.

The heat trapped by the snow makes it easier for mice, voles, and shrews to stay warm, and it even makes their lives easier in another interesting way. As the heat radiating out of the ground hits the snow, it will tend to melt it. But because of the relative humidity of the *subnivean* environment (that's the fancy term for the environment under the snowpack), the ice crystals at the ground level can undergo the process of *sublimation*.

To put it quite simply, the ice evaporates. It goes from the solid state directly to the gaseous state without ever turning into liquid water. This ensures that everything is kept dry, and it also means that the snow at ground level will start to deteriorate into a very fragile, delicate network of crystals that provide the little animals with a lot of room to move around in.

Mild winters provide the small mammals of the forest with little or no protection from cold and predation. The ground is much colder than it would be otherwise, and the absence of snow also means that any little creature foraging for food is going to be out in the open.

On the other hand, these same conditions are more favorable for animals such as deer, turkeys, hawks, and owls. The ground is exposed for the most part, which means that food items such as acorns, hickory nuts, and the small mammals that feed on them are also exposed. If we had three feet of snow on the ground, many animals would simply have to wait, hoping they had stored enough fat to see them through the lean periods.

So the next time you bemoan the lack of snow, remember that you are not alone. You, the white-footed mice, short-tailed shrews, and red-backed voles may all be a little upset, but not, perhaps, for the same reasons.

A muskrat uses a hole in the ice of its pond to get some sun and do a little preening.

The Common Redpoll

Like many naturalists, I keep a field journal. The pages of this book are a patchwork of recordings of the quiet moments that would be forgotten if they weren't jotted down somewhere and the exciting events that could never be forgotten no matter how much time passes. And in between these writings are what I call "the barrens."

These are the days that yield no interaction with nature whatsoever. Summer is a good time for my journal, but September (the beginning of school) is a barren time. October tends to be a better-recorded month because of the undeniable beauty of the season (and my melancholy over the loss of summer), but after the leaves have fallen, "the barrens" return. Eventually comes "the long darkness" of winter, but occasionally Nature sends me a little treat that breaks up the blank pages of the barrens. What follows is an example of just such an entry:

"Every morning, before I leave the house, I go out into the darkness and fill up the feeders on my porch. Every evening, as dark is falling once again, I return home from work to find that the seeds I had offered are gone. I always wonder who has come to dine at my feeders, and I always hope that, whoever my mystery guests might have been, they will return on the weekend for brunch.

"Today is a Saturday, and I was rewarded for my efforts. There was a knocking at my window at dawn (probably a dove at the clear plastic window feeder), and so I got up and put out breakfast. There were thistle seeds for the finches, sunflower hearts for the jays and nuthatches, and mixed seeds for the doves, juncos, and cardinals. Even the crows got some leftover bread from last night's supper.

"I puttered around the kitchen for a little while, and when I looked outside, I saw quite a collection of visitors. There was a young red-winged blackbird, a male brown-headed cowbird, a nuthatch, doves, jays, goldfinches, juncos and . . . believe it or not . . . 30+ common redpolls. All of those free breakfasts were paid for in that one moment!"

The redpolls in particular were of great interest to me that day because they were birds that I had said would be appearing in large numbers that year. Oh how I love being right! This is mostly because it happens with such irregularity. And so, without fear of anything or anyone, I reached for my camera and started taking photos.

A common redpoll feeds on goldenrod seeds.

The common redpoll (*Carduelis flammea*) is a member of the finch family and is very similar in shape and size to its cousin the American goldfinch. In fact, the bird's genus, *Carduelis* (which is of Latin origin) literally means "goldfinch." Where the goldfinch is a beautiful expression in yellow, the redpoll explores the possibilities of reds. The male and female both have a bright red patch on the forehead and a black chin, but in the male this elegant combination of colors is further accentuated by a rosy wash on the upper breast.

Thus, we arrive at the bird's species name, *flammea*, which is a Latin word for "fiery or flaming." When put together, the scientific name of the common redpoll means "the fiery goldfinch." This is one of the better names to be found in binomial nomenclature.

Many winter birds visit feeders to sample the seeds we put out, but for redpolls seeds are a really big deal. Redpolls hold the distinction of being able to withstand colder temperatures than any other songbirds, and seeds are the secret to their success in this matter. A very efficient metabolism allows redpolls to gain body fat during the day so they can maintain their body temperature during long, cold nights. This is a very clever trick, but such small birds living in very cold places may not be able to store enough fat to survive a particularly severe night.

So the redpoll has developed yet another trick. Each bird has an oversized crop in which it can store an extra supply of seeds just before darkness falls. The bird already has a supply of body fat stored up from the day's foraging, but now it also has a crop full of food that it can use as a midnight snack.

The redpolls in the Northeast don't flee from the cold as much as they explore the countryside in search of food. Years that produce deep snow can also cause the birds to move south to areas where natural foods are not buried and out of reach. Food is the driving factor behind the movement of all the winter finches, and redpolls are no exception.

Now the really interesting thing about the flock of redpolls at my feeder was the fact that a member of the flock was noticeably different from the rest. My initial reaction to this sighting was to think that I had found myself a hoary redpoll—another species of redpoll altogether. Upon closer inspection of my photos, however, I decided that my initial reaction to all the white feathers I saw was slightly flawed.

Hoary redpolls are known for their 'frosty' appearance, but the markings on their bodies are fainter overall. The bird I saw had a great deal of white, but also a great deal of that bold streaking on the breast and wings that you would expect from a common redpoll. One photograph in particular allowed me to correct my identification.

The photo actually wasn't that great because the bird had turned its head away from the camera, but the plumage was perfectly clear. For me, the clincher came when I noticed some rather striking asymmetry in the coloration of the wings. This bird was a *leucistic* common redpoll, which is basically like saying it was a partial albino.

A common redpoll.

All winter, during the workweek, I'll keep my feeders stocked with thistle seed in an effort to continue attracting any redpolls that appear. Sunflower hearts might be attractive to the redpolls on a simple "amount-of-food" basis—i.e., how much food each seed represents—but the redpolls have such small beaks that they are challenged to tackle a whole sunflower seed. Millet and thistle seeds, on the other hand, are just about perfect for redpolls.

As winter progresses, I will keep a sharp lookout for any new and interesting birds that come for food. In particular, I look for the appearance of the blackbirds and cowbirds that always seem to arrive much earlier than they should. Either these birds are gamblers, or they are making a big mistake by hanging around for so long, and I always like to figure out which.

I also keep an eye out for the flock of redpolls that visits my feeders almost every winter. Sometimes they make a brief appearance, while others they set up camp for a while, but as long as I keep the feeders stocked they will be less inclined to go looking for something else to eat. I am also very keen to spot a real hoary redpoll within the common flock, but that would just be an extra reward. The darkness may still be oppressive, but the arrival of common redpolls to my feeders will keep the barrens from dominating the feeling of winter.

Voles

Though we may not see them often, wild mammals are all around us. There may be foxes living across the street, a family of coyotes living in the wooded swamp just down the road, or a weasel living in your woodpile, and you may not even realize it. Most mammals, with the notable exception of squirrels, live lives of stealth and are experts at going unnoticed.

Once the snow starts to fall, however, their stealthy ways no longer offer them 100 percent protection from our notice. We may never see the actual animals themselves, but the evidence of their movements is as plain as paint on canvas. We might see where a small herd of deer crossed a road, or where a rabbit spent the night foraging in a raspberry thicket. Suddenly, we all get a chance to catch a glimpse of a world normally hidden from our view. Even under this sort of condition there are still mammals that can hide from us, however. For the most part they are the smallest representatives of their group.

If you have ever heard of a "meadow mouse," then you have heard of a vole. It turns out that the word *mouse* has been used in reference to a wide variety of small mammals for quite some time. So even as recently as 1979, the meadow vole *(Microtus pensylvanicus)* went by the name *meadow mouse*. In general terms, mice and voles are quite similar. Both are small mammals, both are rodents, and both tend to be brownish or grayish in color. Upon closer inspection, however, you will see that there are a few key differences.

In the Northeast, the classic example of a wild mouse is the white-footed mouse *(Peromyscus leucopus)*. It has large eyes, large ears, and a long tail, and it really is kind of cute as long as it isn't getting into your food. It may grow to be 4 inches in length, and it has a tail just about as long as its body. Its main diet consists of seeds, nuts, and insects. In contrast, the meadow vole has smaller eyes, smaller ears that are more heavily furred, and a shorter tail. While a meadow vole may grow to the same 4 inches that a white-footed mouse can reach, its tail (at 2 inches) is only half as long. Basically, you have a shaggier, more compact version of a mouse, and if you are willing to open up your soft side, you will have to admit that voles are really quite adorable.

As similar as mice and voles are, however, there is a key difference in their diets. Whereas mice are seed eaters, voles tend to eat a lot more vegetation. Voles would certainly enjoy delicious

Voles must be constantly alert for predators.

sunflower seeds, or marvelous raspberries, but they also eat a lot of fresh green grasses, the roots, tubers, and bulbs of many plants, the leaves and bark of trees, and even flowers. Voles, if you like, just love a good salad.

Winter is actually a pretty good time to look for signs of voles, but the snow can't be too deep. An inch or two is perfect, but anything more than that will cover the ground too deeply for you to see anything. What you want to look for is a network of raised tunnels in the snow. This may give you the impression of mole tunnels, but at this time of year moles are usually found deep underground, where earthworms (their chief source of food) retreat for the winter.

Surface tunnels, between the ground and the snow, are the work of voles out foraging for green grass shoots. Meadow voles may even build winter nests above the ground as long as there is enough snow to provide concealment. Such a nest is basically a spherical pile of grass cuttings that have been deemed inedible.

There are other voles too. The boreal red-backed vole (*Clethrionomys gapperi*) prefers to live in damp forests of coniferous, deciduous, or mixed tree species. In such habitat there are far fewer grasses to eat, so the red-backed vole adds nuts, bark, mushrooms, and a few insects to its diet. Unlike the meadow vole, the red-backed vole is also a very good climber. Another good climber is the pine vole (*Pitymys pinorum*). Oddly enough, pine voles prefer to live in dry deciduous forests, where they spend a lot of time in tunnels just beneath the leaves on the forest floor. They use these tunnels to safely search for the nuts, roots, and bark of trees, and the roots, seeds, and flowers of other forest plants. I think the name *oak vole* would have been better, but what are you going to do?

Though there are a few small differences between these voles, in coloration and lifestyle, there is one commonality that they all must contend with: voles are food for a great range of predators. Just about any carnivore that can be found in fields or forests will eat voles. Since voles are also quite accomplished swimmers, I am sure large fish occasionally eat them too. To compensate for this tremendous pressure from predation, voles have to breed faster than rabbits do. So let's take a look at the life of an average vole.

Voles may be born during any month of the year. Naked and blind, they nurse for less than two weeks, and they are on their own in only three. At the age of four weeks, a female meadow vole will have reached sexual maturity. Unless she is killed first, she will be pregnant.

She will go off in search of her own territory, which may be as small as one-tenth of an acre, where she will spend the rest of her life. Since predators kill so many voles, however, territories are never in short supply, and the little female may not have to go far to find one.

Her pregnancy will last only three weeks, after which she will give birth to three to nine babies. By the time the babies are weaned, the little female may already be pregnant again. One famous meadow vole gave birth to seventeen litters of babies in one season while she was held in captivity! If she had an average litter of six for each of her seventeen pregnancies, then she had 102 babies in one year!

The problem for wild voles is the fact that the odds of living to the ripe old age of twelve months are not particularly good. Snakes, weasels, foxes, coyotes, hawks, owls, and even shrikes are constantly on the lookout for food, and voles are perfect for all of them. With so many predators, voles can survive only by producing more offspring than the predators can eat.

So the next time you take a walk in a winter field, or even head out to refill your birdfeeders, keep a sharp lookout for the little tunnels made by voles. You never know where these little mammals will appear next, but their presence should provide you with a window into an amazing mammalian community that may otherwise go unnoticed.

The Pileated Woodpecker

Every once in a while, from the depths of the forests to the south of my house, comes the call of a ghost of the forest. It is a sound that I love to hear because it represents a return of greatness to the landscape. At one point in American history Audubon thought this sound might go quiet forever, but now it has returned with gusto. I am speaking of the call of a pileated woodpecker.

The pileated woodpecker (*Dryocopus pileatus*) is the largest woodpecker to be found in the Northeast. With a body length of 16 to 19 inches, this species can fairly be said to be crow-sized (the American crow has a body length of 17 to 21 inches). Like a crow, the pileated woodpecker is also the owner of a largely black plumage. If the bird is at rest on a tree, the coloration that really stands out from a distance is the white striping down the neck. Up closer, the brilliant red crest becomes the obvious feature, and the striping on the neck is revealed to be a more elaborate striping of the face as well. Only upon very close inspection, or with a good pair of binoculars, can you see the color of the stripe that extends downward from the bird's bill. In males this stripe starts off as the same brilliant red of the crest and then switches over to black. In females, this stripe is entirely black. It is only by noting the color of this stripe (also called the mustache) that the sexes can reliably be differentiated.

In flight a pileated woodpecker could never be confused with a crow. For one thing, the shape of the body is completely different. Crows tend to lean toward the stocky side, whereas the pileated woodpecker has a rather smallish head on the end of a long and slender neck. If that weren't enough, you could also take note of the fact that the undersides of pileated woodpecker wings are largely white and their tails are longer and more slender.

Now that we have the identification of a pileated woodpecker out of the way, let's examine the history of this bird and figure out why I chose to refer to this species as the "ghost of the forest." By the time of the Civil War, a substantial portion of the Northeast had been cleared for farmland. At one point

A pileated woodpecker at its drumming tree.

70 percent of southern New England had been converted to agriculture, leaving precious little forest left for wildlife. Many forest species became extirpated, which is a fancy word that means they were driven out of part of their range. Ravens, black bear, wolves, wild turkeys, and even white-tailed deer were faced with the grim reality that the habitats they required simply didn't exist any longer. Pileated woodpeckers had a similar problem.

A pair of pileated woodpeckers requires 150 to 200 acres of forestland for a territory. The size of this territory varies depending on the availability of food and nesting sites. Since these birds depend on trees for food and shelter, it can be said that the size of the territory depends entirely on the condition of the trees within that territory. Ultimately, it is a challenge for any pair of pileated woodpeckers to find all of the proper conditions for living and breeding in a forest.

Food is probably easier to find than nesting trees. Pileated woodpeckers relish carpenter ants and any other insects that live in dead, decaying wood. To get at their prey, they have formidable weapons in the form of their bills. Imagine a pileated woodpecker as a human armed with an axe and you will get the basic idea of how devastating this bill can be to a dead tree. Pileated woodpeckers also chop very distinctive holes into trees while they are looking for food, and they leave large piles of wood chips scattered on the forest floor.

Like that of a human wielding an axe, the attack of a pileated woodpecker on a tree tends to be slow, deliberate, and relatively quiet. After all, the birds are working in one place for an extended period of time, and they may not want to advertise their position to potential rivals or predators. Many people are surprised to learn that the loud drumming of a woodpecker has nothing at all to do with digging holes in trees. If you are willing to stop and think for a moment, however, it makes sense.

The laws of physics apply to woodpeckers in the same way as they apply to humans. If you were going to dig a hole in a tree, you would probably look for softer wood and you would apply force in such a way as to penetrate the tree. If you wanted to make a lot of noise, on the other hand, you would probably look for thinner pieces of wood that would resonate when they were struck (like the bars of a xylophone or a glockenspiel). You would also apply force in a manner that would produce sound and not destroy the wood.

Pileated woodpeckers do exactly the same thing. The biggest problem they face is simply finding trees (either dead or alive) that have sections of wood that have died and cured in such a manner as to produce a resonant tone when properly struck. These drumming trees are important features in a male's territory and often serve as boundary markers. Many drumming trees need to be found around the perimeter of the territory, and the male will drum on them to advertise his ownership of the forest.

The bird I photographed for this essay was perched in a black cherry tree that had been standing dead in my parents' back yard for about five years. That amount of time was needed to allow the wood to dry and cure sufficiently to become a drumming tree, but dead trees in back yards are not always allowed to stand for so long. Excessive management of a small wood lot can actually degrade its value to wildlife, so if you have a dead tree that poses no immediate threat to your house, you might consider letting it stand. Who knows what animals may find a use for it?

Somewhere in the territory there also has to be at least one tree that can be used for nesting. Pileated woodpeckers are large birds, and they need large trees for nest holes. These nest cavities are also highly prized by a number of other forest animals including wood ducks, squirrels, and screech owls. Pileated woodpeckers cannot always drive off competitors, so they often need to excavate more than one nest hole.

With all of these demands, it is easy to see why pileated woodpeckers had such a hard time in southern New England. A ready supply of dead trees is needed for both food and shelter, and then the forest must be allowed to grow unmolested so trees can continue to die over time. The resources needed by the birds shift randomly as time passes because different trees grow and die at different rates. If there are no trees, however, there will be no woodpeckers. When the trees of southern New England were cleared, pileated woodpeckers disappeared and were remembered only as ghosts.

Today, the forests of southern New England are recovering and more and more of them once again contain the larger trees required for nesting. Happily, the pileated woodpecker has also returned to these forests, and it can occasionally be seen flying through the forest rather than just haunting our imaginations.

Wood ducks benefit from the work of pileated woodpeckers.

White-tailed Deer

When I was little, my imagination virtually sparkled with thoughts of Christmas. A Christmas tree covered with lights, ornaments, and tinsel was certainly something that got the blood racing. A plate of cookies and a glass of milk made Santa's imminent arrival even more exhilarating, but for me it was the thought of reindeer that really got me going. Santa's sleigh, pulled by Rudolf and the other reindeer, was Christmas itself.

If I was all a-twitter with the simple thought of reindeer, I can only imagine what my mother must have felt when she was a girl. She grew up in Albany, New York, and lived in a three-story house that had a back porch with an almost perfectly flat roof. I can remember climbing out onto my grandmother's porch roof and dropping water balloons on people, so I am quite certain that the story I am about to relate to you is true.

My grandmother was a naturalist for the Hudson Valley Girl Scout council. My grandfather also worked around animals at his job with the state labs, where he worked on diagnosing rabies in animals that were brought in. My mother's entire family also helped to raise orphaned animals, which included the occasional fawn. Well, fortunately for all of us, little children do not have an overly developed sense of logic. They trust what they see and, for a little while at least, don't understand that adults may intentionally mislead them. So on Christmas morning, when my mother looked out on the roof of the porch and saw tracks in the snow, there was no doubt about who could have made them. Santa had made a visit to the house!

Only years later did she finally come to understand that they had been her father's footprints. He would walk out onto the porch roof with a pair of skis and lay down "sleigh tracks." He then finished off the illusion with tiny hoof prints he made with a stick, and a few well-placed (and very genuine) deer pellets. These pellets were collected from wildlife rehabilitation cages in which young fawns were being housed during the summer and fall. Deer droppings are roughly the size and shape of jellybeans, and, as far as droppings are concerned, they are not particularly offensive or difficult to transport in a plastic bag. So a sprinkling of deer pellets here and there made the scene on the porch roof all the more realistic. The sleigh had landed, the reindeer were present, and Santa himself had walked about while he tended to his deer and checked to see that the children were asleep.

I did not have as elaborate an illusion as my mother, but I did have the next best thing. Who among us doesn't remember watching that old claymation classic, "Rudolf the Red Nosed Reindeer"? I will now admit, some thirty years after the fact, that the abominable snowman frightened the hell out of me. Even though I knew that he became friendly at the end of the show, I was most definitely put off by the menacing figure of the snowman climbing over the mountains. I'm happy to say that today I have made a full recovery.

In retrospect, I think the thing I most enjoy about the show is the fact that it altered the image of reindeer to make them more familiar to those of us who live in the continental United States. We generally see white-tailed deer in our forests and fields, and that is the model that was used by all but the most modern of Christmas moviemakers. It should be noted, however, that white-tailed deer and reindeer are very different creatures. Here in North America we know reindeer as caribou. In northern Europe and Asia, however, caribou were domesticated about 2,000 years ago and are used by many cultures as extensively as the native peoples of the Great Plains used the American bison.

Reindeer differ from white-tailed deer in that both sexes grow antlers. Those of the males (also known as bulls) are much larger that those of the females (cows) and are significantly larger than any antlers grown by male white-tails (also known as bucks). Female white-tails (does) do not grow antlers at all, and both sexes go for many months without them.

I think that many of us have a rather distorted view of white-tailed deer in our minds. We often think of white-tail bucks as being massive and imposing animals that are the lords of the northern forests (probably a result of watching too many Disney movies), but in reality these animals are quite a bit smaller than we might think. A really large buck will stand about 42 inches tall at the shoulder (that's 3½ feet to you and me) and weigh in at an average of about 150 pounds. They are impressive to be sure, but I think that many people have this image of something much

A group of white-tailed deer take a moment to survey their surroundings.

larger in their minds. They are thinking of something more the size of an elk (5 feet tall at the shoulder and 800–1,000 pounds). As with moose, white-tail bucks grow antlers for the purpose of competing for mates, but shed them after the breeding season is over. From January to April there are no antlers on any white-tailed deer. In the spring, however, the males once again start to grow antlers.

Though there are some regional differences in body size and shading, most of the white-tailed deer of North America have the same recognizable patterns in coloration. They have black noses, white chins, black eyes ringed with white, brown bodies, white bellies, and tails that have a brown dorsal surface and a bright white underside. When alarmed, the deer raise these wonderful tails as warning flags, and this is, of course, the source of the animals' name. I said that most white-tailed deer have the same coloration because there are always the occasional albino deer that turn up here and there. Full-blown albinos are rarer than individuals with partial albinism, but white deer are definitely seen from time to time.

From a Darwinian perspective, however, the most interesting deer would certainly have to be one in possession of a red nose. Would the red glow be the result of chemical reactions similar to those found in fireflies? Could it really help Santa to see on even the stormiest winter nights?

This is a very interesting question, and I am sure that many young naturalists will try to stay up on Christmas Eve to see if they can catch a glimpse of a red light in the sky and detect the tinkling of silver sleigh bells. I'm sure they will fall asleep before the big man himself makes an appearance (just as I did when I tried to make such observations), but that won't deter the imaginations of children in the slightest.